Reflections from the Water's Edge

Reflections from the Water's Edge

JOHN BAILEY

The Crowood Press

First published in 1987 by
THE CROWOOD PRESS
Ramsbury, Marlborough
Wiltshire, SN8 2HE

British Library Cataloguing in Publication Data

Bailey, John,
Reflections from the water's edge.
1. Fishing
I. Title
799.1'2'0924 SH439

ISBN 1-85223-080-0

Acknowledgements

Many very deep thanks go to *Angler's Mail* and *Coarse Fisherman* magazine for permission to use the stories previously published in their pages.

I would also like to thank my good friend Martin Smith for help with photographs and, as usual, Chris Turnbull for his sensitive cover illustration.

Picture Credits

Photographs on pages 36, 39, 41, 43, 45, 55, 58, 69, 77, 120, 121, 132, 143 and 153 by Martin Smith; all others by the author
Illustrations by Chris Turnbull

Typeset by Alacrity Phototypesetters,
Banwell Castle, Weston-super-Mare
Printed and bound in Great Britain by
Billings & Sons Ltd, Worcester

CONTENTS

The Last Decade: 1977–1987

INTRODUCTION

Not since I was four years old have I ever been able to go fishing often enough. Even in those summer-long holidays I wanted more. It has always been the same. It still is. I hope it will remain so for ever. And when I have had to return home, so I have wanted to surround myself with all the arts of the angling world. Years and years back, I began my taxidermy collection. If I could not be fishing, at least, then, I could look at fish.

So too with books. 1955 and I was given my copy of *Mr. Crabtree Goes Fishing*. It remains with me – along with another three hundred or more angling volumes that spawn a further twenty or so each and every year. I could not even start to name my favourites. Every one has a position by the bedside at some season or another.

More lately, over ten years perhaps, I have also begun to collect paintings, prints and woodcarvings of fishing scenes. I suppose I could be said to live in angling's old curiosity shop. It is paradise.

This desire both to fish and to surround myself with all fishing's arts inevitably led me into angling writing. My first articles were published in a local paper when I was thirteen. They were written at the back of a maths room when my thoughts were all of big roach on lobworm. From there I moved quickly on to school magazines, university papers and then, in the early 1970s, back to the angling press.

I have never been at a loss to say something. Rather, I have always felt a compulsion to explain what is the most valuable, most cherished part of my life to others. Whenever I get home from the bankside, I have brought with me memories I feel are simply too precious to let go for ever. Not every fishing minute is magic – but very many are.

No other sport offers so many opportunities for the writer. Primarily, there are always techniques to be explained. Newcomers need to know these basic methods, just as more advanced anglers demand to be told of the progressions. But, from this prosaic level, the avenues of angling writing lead into more exotic pastures. Literally. No other sport requires a greater awareness of the countryside in general and the watery environment in particular. No angler merely watches nature in a passive way. He enters into its very existence. He taps all its secrets if he wants to be successful in his quests. The idyll of the fisherman asleep in buttercups, line to big toe, is a nonsense. All anglers work hard as herons for their fish. They have as precise a knowledge of their waterways as a gamekeeper does of his forests. Their expert observations burn to pass on into print, onto canvas, into wood, somehow into the forever.

A mystery unfolded.

Angling, too, is about people. Fishermen are heroes or villains. There are no middling characters, for put a rod into any man's hands and the mediocrity of his day-to-day life seems to melt away. Every angler, alive or dead, deserves his chapter somewhere and has his own tale to tell.

Angling is about tales. Every angler is a master of mystery. His sport is one of legend, history, awe, excitement, drama, tragedy and even humour. Every possibility of the storyteller is open to the fisherman. After all, he is penetrating into an unknown world, seeing secrets well beyond the veil that the shining water puts up before those unfortunates who do not fish.

This collection of stories takes me through thirty years on the waterside. It reflects many of the most marvellous memories of my life, many of my warmest moments.

The Early Years 1955–1970

In some people the urge to fish is irresistible. From their earliest years they cannot help but be drawn by the fascination that water holds for them. This compulsion is so deep, so strong, that it is genetic, I am sure. It comes down through the blood and, though it can miss out a generation or more, it will surface again inevitably.

So, whilst my apprenticeship was served under a hundred tutors, it is to my maternal grandparents that I owe the greatest debt. My grandfather died a quarter of a century before my birth, but my grandmother kept his spirit and his fishing tales alive for me. One in particular fired me when I was only four years old – and came back to haunt me on the death of my parents. In the settling of their estate, I stumbled on a score of memories of that tale ...

Casting a fly line during a misty Pennine dawn.

EDWARDIAN ANGLE

Through recent, sad domestic circumstances, an old case, belonging to my grandfather, came into my possession.

For a long while, affairs were too urgent to allow me the time to look through the contents and, when I did, the photographs and diaries took me weeks to arrange and even longer to absorb fully.

Until then, I had only known my grandfather by repute. A warm, generous man, a Dane whose parents had fled Schleswig-Holstein in the time of Bismarck's persecutions. A man who had had the fortune to die rich, the misfortune to die on Christmas Day in 1935, when he was only in his fifties. But now I know him better and can be proud of him as a great sportsman.

Packs of photographs held together by faded ribbons. Edwardian fishermen, Edwardian fish, old boat-houses, gamekeepers who died in the Great War. Photographs of river keepers in heavy tweeds with the fish they had caught. Letters too, to the great men of the day. Letters from Jardine, Sheringham and the Trent Otter. Discussions on new types of gut, on new spinning reels and a new pike trace. A priceless description from Halford of a golden day on the Test. Yes, grandfather's was a career so rich and exciting, I find it hard to imagine.

It is the diaries that I really love. Forty of them in an unbroken line from the Boer War to the rise of Hitler. Diary upon diary of a fishing man, all caked in dust, with faded gold lettering and occasional frontispieces of Victoria looking as sullen as a pricked chub. There is a volume of stories. Perhaps the one that appeals the most is the diary for 1908.

Grandfather had met the head gardener for the Welbeck Estates and had obtained permission to fish Clumber Lake. In February he went there first. It was a cold day with winds from the south-east and a frost that began to settle in the late afternoon. He had been spinning and taken pike up to fourteen pounds when another fish snapped at his small spoon. A quite different fish from the fight of it and, when it surfaced, he saw a huge perch. The entry for that day closes: 'A yard from the net, I lost it ... I packed and left.'

All through the summer that followed, grandfather fished that lake like a demon: worm, deadbait (no, they are not a modern discovery), small livebaits, spinners and plugs, he tried them all.

Pike, just pike and more pike were all he caught. He killed them and piled his sidecar with them, to give to the Jews who worked in the Nottingham lace industry. There was a depression on, it was before

Jacks for the poor, perch for the taxidermist – the Edwardian angle.

Lloyd George's unemployment acts and they needed food.

But, he saw perch. The dawn of 29 August, a big one followed in the deadbait he was twitching back. He let the roach sink and the perch circled it. The bars and red fins showed clearly in the summer water. The big eye of the hunter gleamed and he made for the head of the bait and shook it as a terrier would a rat. Perhaps he felt the trace. Anyway, the fish stiffened, spat out the silver roach and glided back into the deeper water.

October and it was a mild Sunday. Grandfather was late getting to Clumber. The petrol tank of his motor cycle was leaking. But still, he felt it was worth a couple of hours – and he had promised his friend a visit. Throughout the late afternoon they worked baits across the lake. The pike were feeding well and they had taken over a dozen when a church bell began to ring from somewhere in the park. Could it be so late?

He had promised to collect Maud, his fiancée, my grandmother. They were to sing in the choir at Worksop. But a last cast, an uncharacteristic swift retrieve – and the fish was there again!

The same bulldog head-shaking fight and the big perch that he had pursued all year was his. George netted it for him and they sat and looked at it as the sun sank and the water drained from the net back into the lake. Grandfather had caught his fish and the rest of the memory would linger on quite well without the need to commit it to paper. My grandmother remembered the night well too. She told me about it one evening, half a century later, when she was bedridden and had long since been widowed.

She had been ready quite two hours, all dressed up in her Sunday best. Black lace stiffening, bonnet dusted, probably polished. Upstairs in her room, she had practised the hymns from her prayer book, paced to and fro and asked the maid a dozen times, 'Has Mr Hempel come yet?'

She had received the same reply a dozen times: 'No, not yet Miss, not a sign of 'im.'

When she heard the familiar roar of the Daimler bike approaching the drive, she knew at last he had arrived.

In the dash to the church, they had little time for explanations, but afterwards they drove to the edge of the Dukeries for a while, for it was a warm autumn night. Little was said until Maud, I suspect not always the sedate grandmother I knew, noticed fish slime on her skirt, from the sidecar. So in his defence grandfather told the story.

'We decided then', she told me, 'to have the perch set up. He sent it to Cooper in London! It cost a whole week's wages. Well, when he died, I took it down – it reminded me of him so much. Then, later in the last war, when your Uncle Martin was killed and your Uncle Bill was in West Africa, I thought I might as well be rid of it. I knew your mother wouldn't want it – and none of us knew that you would be along – so I just gave it to the dustman.'

A rare day off the water and on the charabanc.

A four pound two ounce perch! Hmm, well, it's a miracle I got the diaries; who is to say I won't ever get the fish back?

HECTOR AND THE HEROES

Hardly had the sun begun to set over the industrial towns, when a frost began to form. Pillars of smoke rose from chimneys everywhere, big and small, and just froze where they hung. After teatime, the bedroom windows had begun to glaze over from the inside, shivering the moon beams into broken, distorted light. Looking again and again, it was always the same sight – the bare trees, the odd car going past and everyone indoors on a February night.

A child's homework always remains to be done. Boring, horrible job, but best to get it done and leave the rest of the weekend free. Who knows, the weather might turn. It was always worth hoping for – while there are two days off, there has got to be hope.

But Saturday came in still cold. The garden pond had enough ice on it for the birds to stand on, even though the goldfish were visible beneath. Going down to the rec. and the mud in the goal mouth was all torn up and too frozen for a game and there was a blasted north-western fog coming in. Might as well get back. Latin was still to be done, whilst listening to the radio, getting all the latest.

The latest was that the United game was off again: bet Law and Charlton and Best and Stiles didn't have to read about Hector when their game was fogged up. Frost, fog, February – what a wretched muddle-up of a winter it could be.

There was Doctor Who and then the football results. City played in the south and won. Trust them. Upstairs, Hector and Achilles were still kicking about and there was the same bare street and now it was everyone indoors on a February Saturday night. So depressed, elbows on the sill, didn't notice the snow at first, the flurries orange in the neon, the flakes rolled by the wind down the window. Stars had gone. No moon out. Soon came a thaw – a dripping in the gutters and in the downpipes and the occasional car-sprayed slush up at the walls and gates. Windows were condensed and frozen. Going out the back and the pond had a skim of water over the ice. It would be free by morning – Sunday morning.

In the outhouse, the tackle was lying all got ready just in case and it needed only a quick look at the maggots, flick on the reel, glance into the holdall for a recheck.

Hard always, sleeping early on a Saturday night, then, when there were

A boy and his fish.

more cars about, men singing in the streets after closing time, throwing chip papers over the wall. Lying full awake, watching the alarm clock hands go round in the neon-painted light, thinking about the cut, about the swim, about how the wind would be coming down. And would Albert come along at all, later perhaps? Thinking about Albert, sleep came on and the dreams were punctuated with heroes. And roach. Because in the north-west then, if a man said 'fish' he meant roach; life was sticklebacks or roach; there was nothing more or less.

And I wanted roach. I wanted so much to be as successful as Albert that I got up that Sunday at 6 a.m. and got the bike and cranked it along the cobbled lane to the Hatherlow Bridge, hauled it up the grit and wood-board steps to the Peak Forest Canal. The ice had gone and left just the usual sheen of oil slick, and a towpath deep with ruts and mud.

Past the barge basin; over the second bridge which spanned the cart's-breadth nineteenth-century road from the mill, to the rag-bag rows of hands' cottages; past the big houses and down the last dank half-mile to Oakwood Mill I went.

First light was breaking over Oakwood. Nothing bright or cheerful, just a glimmering to let me see the water unfrozen under the far trees, and the damp snow on the branches and on the brickwork and roof of the mill. Deserted now, but for a maintenance man and a guard whose jettisoned, saturated sandwiches still floated where I aimed to fish. Preformed plastic pieces in the water, mill valves still steaming, reflections of the chimney growing brighter as I tackled up. And at 7 a.m. I really was in business and Hector could have turned out for United and Law for the Greeks for all I cared.

I was laying-on double maggot on a size 16 under a matchstick-sized quill – all as light and tight as I could make it, with just a pinch of maggots around the swim from time to time. I was getting sticklebacks all right and one gudgeon, which I thought was a miserable, mottled, smelly old thing after it had made my heart beat for a second.

By midday I was getting panicked, thinking Albert might come and I wouldn't have a roach in the net. I kicked around in the wood, miserable, picked up some bricks from the wall and hurled them at the conker trees and half decided to pack up rather than meet him without roach, when I decided to try again.

The eternal pot of gold – the two-pound roach.

About three, I got my first roach – about two ounces – and into the net it went and I knew I could always pretend I had popped out for an afternoon session only. But as the light failed they just kept coming, those roach, and I was breaking records just like Denis down the Stretford End. Each cast the tiny quill would cock, move three inches against the ripple and go down to the depths and, God, I'd be in again.

Now, I prayed for Albert to come, to see this, to see I could fish, could catch roach. And, at last, his bike sounded in the gloom and I saw him, lit up in the glow of the mill. I tried to act casual, but just couldn't, and when he leaned on the wall behind me to watch, my heart nearly stopped. He netted a fish for me. For *me*. Albert. Albert Oldfield. He applauded when I struck on a hunch and got into a six-ouncer. Albert Oldfield applauded – the man who wrote for the press.

When it came time to pack up, he helped me count the fish, patted me on the back. He patted me, Albert, the hero, and then he sold me a ticket, issued by the County Palatine for one shilling. He got on his bike, pushed off, and called: 'Look in the *Times* come Friday.'

The cutting in the *Times* that Friday read: 'Local schoolboy John Bailey caught twenty roach up to a pound on double maggot at Oakwood Mill.' Reading my Latin that next Friday night was quite bearable: Hector, Albert, Achilles, me and Denis Law were all the heroes now.

A BOY'S FIRST CARP

Teenage years are always unforgettable but perhaps more for the girl who rode in the lakeside field or for the party the night before or for the exam I was supposed to be revising for – all the wrong reasons. So only childhood remains.

No period is more full of rich, great days and their memory will always be vivid and exciting. But there are dangers in their recollection: children's scales are pint-sized and unreliable; nostalgia plays a part in distortion too; some occasions are simply personal and of no great interest to others. One July weekend in 1962 I believe escapes these criticisms.

Ian was an art student who came to visit our house with his parents on a Friday evening. He was, poor man, saddled with me; but the talk turned to fishing, to carp, in which he expressed great interest. In the manner of all eleven-year-olds trying to impress their elders, I regurgitated the stories I had heard of the carp in the local lake. I pretended with great knowledge that I too had caught them in the margins at dusk when the

Swift and sleek – the common carp.

crowds had left. I must have been enthralling, for Ian seemed to believe me and suggested a trip the coming Sunday night. Instant panic. My mother would never agree to my being out late. My lies would be exposed. My new hero would turn away in scorn. She simply looked up and nodded assent.

Saturday was a chaos of preparation: line to buy, hooks to sharpen, a spinning rod to mend and prayers to say. Sunday dawned clear and lengthened into a blistering, still day. Ian would never come, I knew, but he did, and by late afternoon I was packed into his Traveller.

Marple Lakes, that Sunday, was, as it probably still is, the playground of the greater Stockport area. Down the dusty track to the water we passed endless families struggling to and from the various bus-stops. The café was full, the line of one-armed bandits was being cranked limbless, the boats were splashed clumsily over every inch of the lake and over all hung the shimmering heat. And Pick of the Pops – Frank Ifield, I suppose. Adam Faith and the Everly Brothers perhaps, and Telstar I am sure. We each forked out three and sixpence over the high café counter and walked past a million fishermen to the end of the lake.

It is my belief that a man does not change intrinsically between the formative age of seven and death. Circumstances alter, but thoughts and reactions do not. In that long wait for dusk to fall I was quite aware of a pity for the 'noddy', a distaste for the litter lout – but above all of an embryonic attempt to work out the problems I would face ahead. I chose a low-hanging tree, because the darkness would be more intense under it and I would be well hidden by the trunk.

There was an offshoot convenient as a rod rest and I practised a strike or two with the stubby little spinning rod to clear the branches. Ian was away somewhere to my right, apparently still confident of my ability to put a monster on the bank.

Dusk began to come in around 8.30. Alan Freeman and friends departed and the lake began to settle into an extremely still, humid night. A stratosphere of midges hung above in the calm treetops. Bats flickered everywhere against the slate sky. I was in awe. I had never fished so late before and the creeping rats startled me. Trembling, I threw out a handful of crusts and whilst the blackness intensified my fears grew. I was opening my mouth to call to Ian, but remembered my role as expert and swallowed privately.

With piercing suddenness, three horny backs appeared on the fringe of the alder tree. I swung out my own crust and, as the very rings were spreading, as in a fantasy, a dream or a miracle, a mouth broke surface around it and the loops of line went linking out through my fingers.

That strike I will never forget. I had had gudgeon, even Macclesfield Canal roach sputnik through the air to land at my feet before, but I had never met with this wild resistance. Before, I had never needed a slipping clutch and I think that of the Intrepid had long since rusted, so, following no fashion but necessity, I simply backwound.

Ian was by my side with what was now an absurdly small landing net which in the past had seemed absurdly, optimistically large. But we managed, Ian, the net and I, then the carp was on the bank and in my arms. I suppose it was a 300-yard run to the café, over the tree roots, the discarded line and the bread wrappers. The owner was sweeping out, locking up, but he let me put the fish on the scales. Even in those days, five pounds two ounces was not a big carp, but seeing the fish in the glare of the electricity, and feeling its vast golden suit of armour was a turning-point. I lifted my carp to the lake and held it in the margins. For a second I compared it with the tiddlers of my past, still swooning at a fish so big. Then it recovered. Its body worked and its tail splashed putrid water down my arms and into my face and it tasted so sweet that as the bow-wave went I swore I would have to have more.

Mine at last!

Postscript

It was tonight that I realised fully the importance of that long lost summer. I was crouched in the gloom at Gorhall, the carp I wanted had come under the sunken tree and I heard him feed noisily on the surface.

That old, strange, familiar heartbeat, felt in the temples, in the cheeks, the throat. That same all-consuming excitement as fresh as before. As I said, a man does not change. Or, if he does, he is truly aged.

THE PERCHING PIONEER

Today, with the growth of convenience baits, highly efficient methods and all but foolproof tackle, anglers as a breed are in danger of becoming lazy, of overlooking basics. Witness, too, a phone call last night from a friend of mine who had spent the day on the Avon.

He had found a twelve-foot-deep, fifty-yard-long run which he trotted all day for chub. Success was moderate – limited, he realised, by rather

1986, and perch are still a favourite fish for me and Roger Miller.

slack groundbaiting. He trickled loose mash into the swim and much of this was swept right out of range in the fast, swirling water. He admitted that once upon a time he would have taken more care. He used to mould the groundbait around stones and introduce maggots into a central cavity. This method was more work, but it got the bait hard on the Avon riverbed where the chub, roach and barbel really wanted it. His results have fallen along with his efforts. I sympathise. I am slacking myself.

For the first time in years I am fishing very seriously for perch. There are problems, most notably finding good waters in these years after the disease. However, I am pioneering new venues and working hard at the quest. I am even experiencing some success. Yesterday I had a pound fish that was absolutely flawless and gave me great pleasure. I drove home very satisfied with myself until I compared my efforts with those of the winter of 1962/3. Believe me, they pale by any comparison!

That was the year I discovered perching in a reservoir in the north-west. It was a strange bleak place tucked into the Pennines, but the fish were exceptional. They grew large on rich food supplies and the clarity of water gave them a brilliance of colour and marking I found mind-blowing. The fish fought well and took baits eagerly. Hardly surprising, therefore, that I thought perch fishing was bliss itself.

The amount of effort I put into those fish, though, was colossal. It makes my attempts today look very puny.

Each Friday night I got off my train from school and went, brief-case in hand, down to the canal. There, hidden in a drystone wall, I kept a stick made up with line, float and hook. There was also a bucket. In the falling light I kicked around in the leaf-mould for red worms, and then with a couple for the hook I set out to catch perch baits.

It was often seven or eight o'clock before the bucket was full with sticklebacks and gudgeon and then I faced the long tramp home with brief-case and bucket for a very late tea. Saturday and Sunday both would see me up an hour before dawn facing a five-mile bicycle ride to the water with gear and bait buckets strapped to the frame.

Often the weather was atrocious, but I went nonetheless, and always stayed until darkness fell once more. I knew dawn and dusk were the best perch taking times, and I was not going to miss either of them.

I took tremendous care over my whole approach, even to the point of pioneering a new perch groundbaiting technique. I had bought a large thick-walled goldfish bowl and I whittled a huge cork slab to fit it tightly. I filled the bowl, the size of a football, with water and put in about twenty sticklebacks and gudgeon. In went the cork stopper and, attaching the bowl to a rope, I threw it into my swim.

My idea was that the bowl would act as a type of attractor, or groundbait. It worked! In the clear water of the reservoir, you could see the perch gather around it and peer at the captives inside as if they were watching a submerged TV set. I swear you could hear them lick their lips on hungry days, and a bait dropped nearby would be snaffled at once.

Early in 1963, the worst weather for decades hit Britain. The reservoir took the easterlies rolling down the Pennines and froze for some six weeks. But, so great was my passion, I would not be stopped in my quest. All that February a fourteen pound lump-hammer became an essential part of my equipment. It took its place in the wall to break the canal ice on the Friday night. Then, along with bait and brief-case, it was carried home to commence duties on Saturday morning.

At the reservoir, I tied a rope to its shaft and flung it out again and again until a channel was cleared for five yards out. I could fish over water fifteen feet deep and I caught perch as easily as I had done in November. More easily in fact. I found that the shoals were attracted by the sound and by the increased light and oxygen.

Often, though, I was in severe pain. There were no thermals then and in temperatures well below freezing my woollen gloves would become wet and would soon freeze to my very fingers. I remember a particular dour afternoon, interrupted by flurries of snow, when I cried from the

Perch – a wonder at any age.

Fruits of a summer dawn.

agony of the cold, landed a perch and began to laugh from the bitter-sweet ecstasy of it all.

I had to stop, though. One day I lost my lump-hammer. Its rope snaked unnoticed around my leg and as I threw it so I followed it in a graceful arc into the water. The lump-hammer pulled me down and for a frightening ten seconds I knew exactly how those gudgeon and stickle-backs in the goldfish bowl had felt.

I hauled myself out and cycled homewards. My clothes froze hard as armour plating, my hair spiked up like a hedgehog, and, hammerless, my perching was done for the season.

THE PHOTOGRAPH

If a fishing photograph should become lost, no hiding place could be more appropriate than within the pages of an old copy of *Still-Water Angling*. I had all but forgotten that I owned the book even and to re-read vintage Walker was alone a pleasure, but when the faded picture fluttered to the floor my delight grew.

What a trigger to memories that photograph was to be. As soon as I looked at it the long-ago day flooded back with all the warmth and triumph I had felt over twenty-two years before. I was barely a teenager then, in July 1964, little more in years than the carp I cradled had weighed in pounds. Eleven pounds six ounces it went on the Samsons – my first double and only my second leather carp. That fish, that day, were both long-term highlights in my early career.

It was just after sunrise when I arrived that day, and already the summer air was milky warm. Mist hung over the lake and a heavy dew was on the valley and I can easily remember that tense anticipation in my breast as I stumbled down over the cattle pasture. As was usual, I made base camp on a small island and then inspected the reed margins and the top shallows before starting to fish.

At the head of the lake, in the cow drink, I saw a fish, bubbling and blowing – 'smoke-screening' was the term of the day, if I remember. A worm would have served me better, I suppose, but I determined to try him on crust. I wriggled up to a lakeside tree and, once hidden, flicked the bait out into the bay. The water was so shallow and so clear the carp made instant moves towards it. He swirled twice and then made a good round mouth and sucked hard. The line snaked. The Chapman cane Mark IV buckled round and stayed well bent throughout the whole thrashing contest.

Faded testimony to the first double.

He weighed two pounds eight ounces. He was a lovely mirror carp and I walked back to the island singing merrily as I always used to in those youthful days of success. Oh yes, a glorious morning – but my day had hardly begun.

The hours stretched to a noon of shimmering heat. Dragonflies, doves in the park and the carp in the lake began to siesta. I drank a lemonade and climbed around in the rhododendron trees, looking down into the shade-dappled water beneath. First, small roach and perch took shape, then dead branches – then *it* swung into view.

No doubt in my mind, *this* was the biggest fish I had ever seen. There, king of the jungle, he felt safe, the untouchable one. He wallowed, he bubbled, he blew, he chuckled the day away a yard below me. He was the first fish I had ever stalked at close range and I think I realised all the risks I was running.

I checked my gear, selected the very best lob from the tin and worked back into position. I watched him once more and went through a battle plan in my mind. No good. If I hooked him I would have to go in.

I eased back, put on my waders, and shuffled back to the rod. The worm landed ten inches from his purple-blue snout and lashed around in the clear water.

The carp watched the worm and I watched the carp. My heart beat in my brain. My mouth was dry and I realised that this was the real fishing I had dreamed of. This was the birth of a specimen hunter.

Over half an hour passed, minutes of excruciating bliss, before the carp moved purposefully to sip in the much-quietened worm.

The result I can look at now – the photograph is all I have for the details of the fight were too blurred, too frenetic to etch deep in the memory. A vague impression of wading ashore, carp in the net, is all I can muster these twenty years on.

I was still there at sunset when the adult members came onto the water. They used floating crust, or worms, flake and potato, close in under floats. There was all manner of rods and reels on show, a lot of talking and laughter and the feeling that no one took carp that seriously.

I had my third fish, margin-caught amongst the rushes. The line caught around the reel handle on the carp's first rush and I was pulled off my log into the slime. The men crowded around and hauled me and my carp clear. Six pounds five ounces. Another mirror. They towelled me down and gave me some swigs of coffee. I sang to myself all the rest of the evening as happy as any boy can be.

That's how my carping was at the beginning, as fresh and as lovely as only youthful pleasures can be. Carp fishing itself was in its infancy then. There was little or no tackle snobbery – Mark IVs were desirable but not obligatory and there was rarely need for the very long-distance work of today. Then there were few special baits or methods and watercraft was the important element to master.

Of course, the carp were not as big in the early sixties. That eleven-pounder which made me a hero then probably would not be weighed now. Size, though, is not everything and the friendliness everywhere on lightly fished waters made the sport very special.

FISHING IN THE LOST AND FOUND

Yesterday I saw a pike that I lost nine years ago. I missed him again now, and, unless fate decrees otherwise, he is gone and I will not see him any more. This hurts because he is a fish I have wanted for nearly thirty years. But at this stage I had better explain further.

No longer a boy's dream – Roger Miller returns a twenty-pound pike for the author.

Like every good boy of the 1950s my angling reading began with the tales of Mr Crabtree. He and Peter guided a whole generation of anglers and I know for a fact that many of the big names of today still look over their shoulder to that world of peace, of beauty and success that Bernard Venables created for us.

It was not so much what the book taught that mattered, but the spirit of what he drew and wrote was inspirational. Everything, always, was wonderful in the Crabtree world. The tench were red-eyed and chubby, the carp were sleek, free-biting commons, the roach averaged a pound and a half and the pike were unmarked, and the bream even bubbled when they should. There was no litter on the banks. The sun generally shone. Dawns were misty and full of promise and the sunsets looked golden, studded with swallows.

No wonder I loved the book, or that it took over on my bedside table for so many years, where, if anything, the low lamplight dusted it with even more mystery and anticipation. Page 23 was my special favourite. I have it here now.

We are in the winter section of the book. Mr Crabtree and Peter are about to go livebaiting for pike, for this giant fish that is snaking through the reeds and hits into the roach shoal that scatters off the top and the side of the page. As often as not, twenty-five years ago, it was that page that I would fall asleep by, it was that fish that would stay with me through the night. The chiselled head, that evil eye, those iron-clad gills and that mighty body forever screwing upwards in a lunge of desperate power could never let me alone. Whenever I was by water that too was deep and sinister, I always hoped he was close by.

So it was that pike fishing the winter through became my favourite – always with plugs and spinners, on canals and ponds. Always cold, often wet, never with more than a jack, I never begrudged Peter his fantastic successes. Rather they kept me going, as though one day I hoped I would become a Crabtree myself.

Nine years ago I was setting up home, browsing through an out-of-town antique shop for odd pieces of furniture, when in a back room I came face to face with Him, that childhood hero, the Pike. He was as large as I had always dreamed – twenty-eight pounds, caught from the Thames in 1917. He had been set up by Cooper, the greatest ever fish taxidermist, who had exactly the same vision of him as had Venables, the greatest ever storyteller. The only difference that I could see at once was that the roach had managed to escape from page 23 and had been replaced in the case by six little Thames dace, one of which lay buckled across those mighty jaws.

I was bewitched. The colours of the heaving flanks, the angle of upward lunge, the deadly menace of the whole scene were exactly from the book. The pike had risen from the page.

I knew at once that I could do without tables and chairs if I could have my fish. But he was sold. I had lost him by a day. I contacted and pleaded with the new owner, a dealer looking only for investment and profit with no eye to art or the fish's immortality. All he would consent to do was to notify me if he ever decided to sell and, as you would expect, I never heard from him again.

And so finally to yesterday, when the story repeated itself, when I found the pike in a Norwich taxidermist's shop, half hidden by owls, bear skins and some poor native's shrunken skull. He was more grand than I remembered him; the bull-like thickness around his shoulders I recognised from some of the pike I have captured now as a man. His fins were perfectly mottled, his flanks expertly flecked, and, whilst I could never kill a pike and believe the natural is always finer than what man can do with glass and plaster, I still yearned for that fish.

But the case had 'sold' labelled on it once more. Still he was not mine. Yet, this time, it was easier to leave the old boy. I feel our paths are destined to join and he will take up his place by my bedside again.

HOW I CAME BACK TO ENGLAND

Up in the barn, in an ancient tub that once stored the farm's potatoes, stand my discarded rods. They always look sad to me, like cast-off loves, once the cherished centrepieces of sunsoaked days and now cast like nuns into shadow and cobweb. It shames me to say that my Chapman Mark IV rests out his days there now, for once he was the closest of friends.

He was bought around twenty years ago, for about £5. For the money, he was the best split-cane carp rod on the market. The splendid B. James version I could not afford until some years later.

The Chapman and the James versions of Walker's immortal rod differed in one important feature: the Chapman had a detachable butt. Now this did not destroy the rod's action in any way and it did mean that the break-down carrying length was only about four feet rather than the five feet of the James rod.

For this simple reason, the Chapman became my travelling rod for many years. I found that with a Mitchell 300 and a small box of floats, leads and hooks he would serve me for almost all eventualities.

So I entered my teens and the late sixties when new experiences and far-flung travels seemed essential. Nearly all the stamps in my passport date back to those Merseybeat days and the Chapman went with me just about everywhere.

He caught carp in Holland and France and Italy, lost a barbel in Spain and bent into chub from here to Germany. His last adventure proved nearly fatal, though. He was rested. That was years ago.

In 1970 I was living in Nice on the French Mediterranean coast. I had a room in a shabby hotel and worked night shift as a kitchen porter in a pizza bar. I finished in the early hours and would take a drink or two in the cafés of the old town, overlooking the harbour and the gently rocking sea.

Even at 2 a.m. the winds there seemed always soft southerlies that whispered of Africa and smelled of salt and the inshore fishing fleets that used the harbour there. Sardines, herrings, anchovies, whitebait, I know not what, but their heads and their guts each evening went into that lime-green water that washed the sea walls.

And each morning, as I strolled round for coffee and croissant, I noticed that the white corpses had gone, had been swept mysteriously away under cover of the light Mediterranean night. The tidal range was only a foot or two and the harbour lapped like a bath. I could not believe that underwater currents had carried them away.

I made enquiries amongst the old men who mended the nets and made the lobster pots and amongst the even older women who cleaned the fish and learnt that the scraps were eaten. They were taken by fish of the night, by sea snakes, by great eels that prowled the boulders and refuse of that ancient harbour bed.

The Chapman was got ready with 10-pound line and a size 2 carp hook. I begged three plump sardines from a Genoese boat, stashed them all at my usual seafront café and left for work.

I remember it was a steaming night, perhaps too humid for eating. The restaurant was quiet. Odd couples came in after the theatres closed but there were none of the large parties that were happy to drink till dawn. I got away at midnight, down the side alley that gave onto the quayside.

I chose a place by old carved steps that led right down into the water itself. I had no net and hardly knew what to expect, except that it would have to be beached and lifted out. I cast a head-hooked sardine ten yards into the oily, welling water and the line peeled off as it fell twenty feet through the semi-phosphorescent depths.

I flicked the bail arm back and hung one of the café's white paper serviettes over the line, large enough for me to see it from my pavement table.

Even a port has a quiet time. At three the café closed and I was alone on the quayside but for the inevitable beggars of those parts wandering in and out of the alleyways. I had made two casts and was onto my last sardine. Dawn was not far away. The skies were brighter over the rocky outcrop at the harbour mouth. The sea was coloured deep lemon and the lights of ships far out seemed less clear.

Soon, there were cars in the old town and a buzz of traffic over the headland down the Promenade des Anglais. I was tired. I had had too much wine. My only prospect was a fitful sleep in a room that was too hot, over-noisy and reeked of stale food.

But, and this is the wonder of fishing, at this low point the serviette twitched, pulled along the quarry stone and fell off the line into the oil-slicked water beneath. Line spilled relentlessly off the spool and vanished away into the mist-hazed harbour water.

I hit it with all the Chapman had. A cloud of silt, green at first, bloomed upwards fifteen yards from me and as it enlarged its colour deepened to khaki brown. It never left the bottom. It twisted and corkscrewed there for hell itself.

The sun was up. Two early-morning workers stopped by me. Twenty minutes passed and then we saw the silver belly of an eel working away desperately deep down. I piled the pressure on the Chapman to keep it out of the rubble and off the anchor ropes. For the first time I noticed the rod groan like a suffering animal in my hands.

With the fish four feet down, it looked five feet long, sometimes on its back and sometimes still trying to escape backwards down to its tangled lair again. As I saw the creature's eyes, the hook pulled free. It had been quite straightened out.

I ate an ice cream and, looking along the Chapman, saw that it was bent like a banana. Strangely, though, for the first time in years, I felt homesick. Within a week, I was fishing at dawn again, on a reed-fringed lake for bream. That is how an eel brought me back to Norfolk.

Back on a summer lake once more.

Fruition
1970–1973

When I returned to Norfolk, I wondered how I could ever have stayed away. After city life, the countryside was a promised land. I threw myself into a rural life. I worked on farms, then as a worm digger, a reed cutter, and even with the longshore fishermen. Nature entranced me. I began to shoot, to watch coastal birds and of course, I continued to fish with an escalating passion.

My patch in the north of the county was an enchanted place and I travelled constantly to know it and its hidden secrets. I walked every mile of the Rivers Wensum, Bure, Glaven and Stiffkey. I haunted the marshes, winter and summer, and I explored every pit, pond and lake. I saw beauty everywhere I looked, both on the coast and in the country. I felt awed by the wildness of the sea marshes and humbled by the elegance of the country estates. Each new day brought a fresh fascination and I had never been a half so happy in my life before.

THE LOST SIXTEENTH

Only once in more than twenty-five years have I missed the opening night of the coarse fishing season, and then I was sick to my heart. Yet it was my own fault. I did not have to go to London, to a party. I chose to meet up with old friends, old loves, and to turn my back on Billy and Joe who I knew were beginning on Bayfield Lake.

The decision was mine alone, and yet evening long I regretted it and yearned to be back in Norfolk. The party was full of noise, of music from the sixties; it flowed with wine and spirits. The people there had once all meant a lot to me for a hundred different reasons but still that long thin lake and those two good country boys pulled all my heart-strings.

I walked with a girl I knew into the garden, a precious place with a swimming pool and the heavy smell of flowers. We stood in the shadows and all I could think was how grand a night it was for fishing. There was only a murmur of wind and a skim of cloud covering a half-moon. It was warm and still enough to hear the bats fluttering after the moths pulled to the party lights.

In my mind, I could see Bayfield clearly enough and imagine Billy and

Friends: a carp and a lovely summer pool.

Joe beneath the blackness of the trees, sitting either side of the outfall on the dam. It would make water music for them all night long, until the dawn broke and the tench began to feed in earnest. Then, as the bubbles burst and the floats began to stir, they would forget everything else, me included, I knew.

How well I knew the rush of a Bayfield tench, hooked and furious, and how deeply I loved their beauty and their olive-soft skins. Run your fingertips along their flanks and it was like touching silk. Yes, silk exactly, like the feel of the dress now between my arms.

It was 12.05 a.m. and I fingered my bow-tie and cursed softly. I insisted we leave the party for a while. We were on the Thames, in a high part of the town, and from the street outside we could see the river beneath. It was cocooned in lights. Tilleys burned on both banks as it wound away like a glow-worm into the night.

I realised that we made a strange sight, walking along the towpath in dinner jacket and long trailing gown, but I hardly think anybody there noticed. The new season was, after all, only fifteen minutes old and fish were being caught.

We came to a lock where a man was playing a bream. I netted the fish for him and settled under the umbrella, landing more as they came. The girl fell asleep on a bench and we covered her with my jacket and his Barbour and continued to fish well past dawn.

There was a holiday atmosphere down the river that night. The reflected swinging Tilleys painted everything in carnival lights. I felt a part of the occasion. As an exiled fisherman I was made fully welcome. I even cast and hooked and landed a couple of dace myself whilst my adopted angler drank from a bottle I had spirited from the party.

It was, I suppose, an opening night at second hand but by morning I had mud on my shoes, groundbait on my shirt frills, bream slime on knife-creased trousers and I was happy at last. The girl awoke, tired and frozen, and I took her for a coffee in the town. She obviously could not understand a fisherman and thought me quite mad. I never met her, or that kind fisherman by the lock, ever again.

I have never jeopardised my opening night since then. It has become quite sacred. It is a glorious mix of long-laid plans, untried places and big-fish dreams. Even to feel the tackle again is special, full of simple thrills. New line looks fresh on the spools and is for once that exact sixteenth of an inch beneath the rim. The rods look good, rewhipped or at least revarnished and attractive once more. There is a collector's joy in opening a tackle box that is all sorted, restocked and raring to go.

And, of course, everything is so marvellous because of the anticipation. You have had time to think everything through and to savour every last thought. The excitement has kindled and grown and become so intense that it almost bursts within you. It is a feeling you know and I know but is lost on some girl on a park bench all damp with the dew and who has never heard of the Glorious Sixteenth.

JOB ON THE LINE

Summertimes, I used to work on the farm that now borders us. This is how I first saw our present house fifteen years ago and fell in love with the place. The estate manager then was a fine sort of chap who well understood my passion for fishing. He could not really be in any doubt of it: at lunch I would make for the farmyard pond to eat my sandwiches over the ready made up rod; in breaks, I dug for worms in the ditches and along the meadow heads where we were working.

The river's the place to be ...

My job was to operate the potato-harvesting machine, and hot, tiring days they were amongst the billowing dust and horseflies. Sometimes, though, it rained, perhaps enough to soak through the topsoil and to bog down the heavy machine. All we could do then was to wait for better weather to dry the land off once more and I would be sent to the cowsheds or to pick wild oats from the cornfields.

One gloomy, wet morning, however, as we sat under the steadily dripping awnings of the machine, the manager told me to go, to get fishing for the day. The one rule was, though, that I had to be back at 4 p.m. if it cleared, in case he wanted an evening start.

A planned holiday is always good, but an unexpected one is a thousand times better and the van fairly skipped along the wet lanes hung over by the drooping cow parsley and the sodden honeysuckle.

I made for a watermill that I had found, long abandoned, its whitewash flaked, its walls half tumbled down, but where a deep, clear pool ran slowly beneath. Very isolated it was then and I believed no one ever fished there. The path, overgrown with nettle and loosestrife, testified as much and I could feel that it belonged to me, my own private place.

I mashed up a little flake and threw it into the head of the pool, into the trickling sluices. Then I put up roach gear and began to lay on under the rod tip with a red quill. Yellow flag was all around and I peered out from under the branches of an elderflower tree, content at last with the day.

There is a Beatrix Potter children's character, a frog called Jeremy Fisher, who goes out over a river on a lily-pad boat to fish for minnows. The illustration that accompanies it was in my mind then – all streaky greys and watery greens. I could even feel the rain running down his back and into his galoshes. Soon my lunch was as soggy as his butterfly sandwiches, but it was, of course, the perfect day for big fish. Just as Jeremy himself found out. He was eaten by a trout.

First, there were bursts of pinhead bubbles as the roach shoaled in and soon the float began to tremble then, half cocked, it slid away to the first fish. Hours passed and roach after roach came out of that little pool amongst the reeds. Work, I felt, had never been so good.

In the early afternoon, though, it began to brighten. Bands of blue appeared in the sky. The birds became more active, doves flew in and out of the mill loft and, sure enough, a blazing summer sun soon rode high.

The rushes began to dry and smoke in the heat, and I knew my holiday was abruptly over. The church clock at G. struck three. I had a fifteen-minute walk, a forty-minute drive and I knew it was time to be on my way.

I emptied out my bucket, took down my nets and turned to deal with the rod. It was buckling in the rests, its tip curved deep into the water.

The reel clutch was rasping. There was no striking and whatever this was it had taken me well downstream, to the tail of the pool. I followed it, stumbling through the marshy ground, and all the while the minutes flew.

A roach rod could make little impact on this fish, a strange fellow for a small stream. Ten past three. My job, not the fish, was on the line. Another minute, and two, then I clamped down, gave it everything and up, up it came, smooth as a rifle barrel, a paddle-finned tench. A full twenty seconds I gave myself to look at her, watching the full sun sparkle and dance down her lateral line to that eye, red-ringed with rage.

The tractor had started, the gang was on board and everyone was at his place. Down the furrow I hared, at my position on the sacks as the first potato was ploughed from the earth. The manager walked to the hedge and nodded and ever since I have owed him my first five-pounder.

THE TOLLBRIDGE POOL

If ever a place reeked history, it was the Tollbridge Pool as it was then, some twenty years ago. An old lane led to it, branching from the straightened modern road that bypassed the former dog-leg route. At the pitted track's end stood the red-brick cottage that was once the toll-house. Here fares were collected on the carts about to cross the river by way of the humped bridge. That bridge still remains, and the big pool beneath used to give me such fine days with the rod.

Fishing cost a shilling – five pence today. The coin was left on the mat and sometime during the day the door would open and the ancient tollkeeper's horny hand would swipe up these latter-day tolls. My shillings were never wasted. A net of roach and dace could be guaranteed by float fishing the tail of the pool where the river began to narrow once more and deepen between beds of thick sedge. And if I cared to put a pike bung out in the slack at my feet a run or two would always come before daylight was out.

The shilling also included tea, sometimes five or six times in the session. The door would creak open and sure enough the tollman's head appeared over the parapet, and then along the hedgerow that gave to my swim in the rushes. The brew was invariably foul – strong and thick with sugar in a cup at best grimy – but always I drank it and listened to the old chap's tales.

He was a Great War veteran and had fought with a Norfolk regiment on the Somme. On one of those manic rushes across no-man's-land, the

The bridge over the sparkling water.

The old man's countryside river.

tollkeeper was the only man of his platoon to be left standing when the smoke cleared. He told me this same story every Sunday for two years and yet it never lost its own vivid drama. Over and over the man relived his nightmare. Fifty years on his eyes still widened with disbelief that he was still alive, intact when those around him draped the wires no better than stoats on a keeper's line.

It is my shame to admit this now, but the pike I caught those days we killed, the old man and I. They were jacks nearly all and he had come to depend on them as a feast, as a boost to a pension miserly small for a hero.

At dusk, he took the small fish into his cottage and the oven chimney would begin to smoke. After packing, I always stopped in for a last pot of tea and watched him scurry around for parsley, butter and sage – anything to flavour the muddy flesh of the pike from a small, slow river. All the journey home, the scent of that bizarre kitchen lingered in my nostrils as the day's brew-ups began at last to churn in my stomach.

The day came when I left the shilling piece and, though I knocked, it was not collected in. I fished all through the short February afternoon and had a great bag of fish moving on to the tail of the pool to spawn. The congregation of dace had attracted pike and I had my biggest ever from the river. It pulled the Samsons down the full fourteen pounds and, as the fish swung in the pale light, I heard a knocking on the upstairs window pane of the cottage.

A curtain was drawn back and there stood the old man grinning, thumbs up, beckoning me in. There was no fire downstairs. The oven was cold. I was called up the stairs to where the tollkeeper lay abed, very weak. That day I made him the tea and left him the pike to be prepared by a woman from the village. Then I bade him farewell.

The following week, the shilling was not collected at all. By March, a pile of the silver coins stood on the mat and the cobwebs fell over them. When I returned in June, the cottage was boarded up and the garden was amuck with weeds. The tollkeeper had gone on at last, after cheating death for near on half a century from that hellish Somme dawn.

Always, I think of the tollkeeper these last days of winter and I still fish around his house to make the most of the migratory dace and roach. Great sport can still be had – why, it was only in 1985 that I took three two-pound roach in consecutive casts from the reflection of what was once the old man's kitchen window. There are pike there too and, needless to say, they now go back unharmed.

I say 'once the old man's window'. Today, the cottage is a rather smart restaurant, patronised by the better off in the county. Extensions have been made. The potholes in the lane have been filled. The garden has been swept away to provide a car park for the guests.

But not everything has changed at the tollman's cottage. Look on the menu outside and you will see for sale 'Filets de brochet'. Fillets of pike then are still eaten in the house, but for a price that must make the tollkeeper's ghost chuckle every time the bill is made out and the cheque card flutters on to the plate. Remember he got his pike for nothing, with a shilling a day thrown in to heat the fire!

MEN OF THE LAKES

There was Tom at L.F., and Ernie on the Causeway and Nick on the Marsh; there is Len at Kit's Lake, Don at the Deer Park and Ted at the Mere, and the list could go on. They are Norfolk waterkeepers, not of the trout streams but of the lakes and pools where rudd, tench, carp and pike thrive.

They are men of the past in some ways. They represent stable societies, where the landed estate guaranteed a good man a job, a home and a place in life. They reflect a golden period, before the insecurity and unem-

Waterkeepers, often gamekeepers too, proud of their fox lines.

No water survives without work.

ployment of the modern age stepped in and cast us all into the role of fugitives from the dole office.

They are men of cottages – small, red-bricked, pantiled places always near water. They are eighteenth- or nineteenth-century homes, built when the estates flourished and spread to anything up to 25,000 acres in extent. The cottages always have gardens, a neat quarter-acre given over to bedding plants and vegetables in equal proportion. The fences are painted, there are roses and honeysuckle around the porches and wisps of smoke always trail from the chimney pots.

Waterkeepers have dogs and these are always either labradors, black or golden, or spaniels. They are shooting dogs with tender mouths and good noses, yet still able to hunt a rat or dig up a mole or two. The man and his dog will never be seen apart, as if both have equal right to the life that they enjoy.

These are men a rung above the ordinary land-labouring class. They wear a jacket, and generally a tie, and they will never go without shaving. They were brought up to talk to the master, to his friends and any of the gentry on the autumn shoots. Their corduroy trousers will always be tucked into waterboots, and they carry either a stick or a gun.

I am talking about men with special skills, with handed-down knowledge that could date back to their great-grandfathers. They know about the rhythm of life in their great parks and they care about it, and will help when they can. Trust them to know where the owls roost, or where the waterhens lay and even if a badger should be about.

Waterkeepers are men of tales, who draw round the lakes on the long summer evenings when the pigeons clap their wings on the dive and the swallows feed until ten or later. The stories tell of big fish caught and lost, of past heroes and of natural phenomena, of the grebe eaten by the pike or the carp that fed amongst the toads at spawning time.

You might think that the keepers' tales exaggerate, but rather I call them optimistic. They sincerely believe that there are rudd bigger than have been caught and that there are tench with dorsals the size of a man's hand.

Certainly, it is not hard to make friends with a waterkeeper. They harbour no jealousy, for who could lead a better life than they? They would never steal or cheat, for what more in life have they to gain? They are men of advice and their houses are always shelter from the storm.

One July dawn I fished from the meadows at Oolerts with the island before me, and the boat-house and the water-trailing woods a hundred yards to my left. The night had been humid but a slight temperature drop in the early hours had resulted in grey mists rising here and there like shrouds off the water.

The beauty of an estate lake.

A great carp took the bait I had out for tench and on the light line he rode just where he wanted to. I made no impression on him – my rod could have been a reed for all the control I had over him. After some minutes, the leviathan took it into his head to surge down the pool, westwards towards the snags of the forest and the boat-house piers.

I tried to make him fight every inch of the way, but really I knew I was losing. Line went off the spool in shrieks that almost broke my heart as the branches of a sweeping oak tree loomed nearer and nearer to the fleeing fish.

My hand clamped down over the clutch and the ninety yards of nylon stretched and whined to the tension. The fish boiled massively at the very tips of the green wooden fingers and inch by inch thrashed towards their touch. I shut my eyes and my prayers thudded in my brain.

Here I was, on the fisherman's precipice, when from the woods rained large flints that landed exactly between the carp and the stretching branches. Alarmed, bemused, the fish turned and wallowed and all but gave in. Minutes later, the waterkeeper, my saviour, was by my side to net him safe.

This summer, I tell this tale for him, and for all the good men of his type.

THE GREY GHOSTS OF CRIPP'S ISLAND

On the eve of his wedding, on the eve of my finding those Felbrigg rudd, Cripp came to my rescue. He knew of my search, as did all my friends at that time. He knew that I felt I had to catch a wild creek mullet and, though I was always first a coarse fisherman, a fish is a fish; and a challenge is a challenge. It was a task that had started in late May, and I was still at it come July. It was also the time I realised that it is not the catch so much as the catching that counts, and though I had had mullet in plenty from the Gorleston quayside, where they gathered by the food factory outfalls, I could not give a damn about those. A creek fish that comes with the tide and flies with the ebb, a fish that feeds off plankton and mud scums, a fish that travels the sea routes like a gypsy is a goal for any fisherman, coarse or not.

I called it the Enchanted Coastline, east of the Wash and west of Yarmouth, a land of bays and sandbanks and tangles of creeks. I had a boat that summer and near lived in it, spending nights away from home, wandering with a load of tackle, sleeping in sand dunes, swimming at dawn, with a pint or two on the way and some friends made and lost.

The never-ending lonesome creeks.

I came close to mullet. You could always find their tracks all right, where their lip marks showed like tram lines on the drying mudflats. But wait on the incoming tide and they would sense you; or the wind would be wrong, and on a whim they would be on their way dancing up another creek. And you would be left, dug in amongst the lavender, wondering what the hell, walking back to the boat and spitting at the stars.

I had stumbled on a hole where the mullet had come in four tides running. The marks were always fresh and I had baited well with bread and slops. An hour before sun-up I was there. Oyster-catchers were walking the muds, peewits were wheeling white in the black and the sea was a mile away, but still I staked things out; put up the thirteen footer; Mitchell and three-pound line; float set for two feet; a size 12 for a lump of flake. I lay back, chewing on the samphire, that rich green marsh asparagus that clears a tired head. I watched the east grow pearl and burning red. I turned west and saw the tide push down the creek and start to glow as it poured into the path of the sun.

In the tongues of water, the mullet came in with fast furrowing bow-waves, sometimes jumping clear, now at my feet, where the bread was soaking, drifting with the water. The swim, mud twenty minutes before, was now alive with fish and, trot after trot, I followed the quill into the sunrise. Two crabs apart, it never deviated, though I fished till the last ebb, till all the mullet had gone seaward past me once again.

I docked at breakfast time, Friday. Cripp was on the quay; the next day was his wedding. We both looked rough – lack of sleep, drink, that sort of thing. I told him my story; he told me his and a sorry one it was, for both of them, it seemed to me. For him I had no solution but to grin and be married; for me, he suggested a mullet pool, an acre of water in a sandspit two miles out. We agreed to meet early, to catch the tide and be back by church time.

So, at 2 a.m., Saturday, I was up. A lovely, warm night it was, with a dust of stars and the slightest breeze. Way before light, we set out down the channel and made it into the pit, a great sheet of water sheltered from the open North Sea by a spit of shingle and sand. We passed its point and nosed into the surf of the true sea, and then turned west, following a route through the sandbars.

As the sun rose we passed Seal Island, and the coal-black eyes watched us pass. Teddy bear faces. The colours grew, the sea birds became white, the sky blue and the sand settled down deep gold.

I thought again: it is not the catch, it truly is the catching; and that I had never been closer to heaven. In that purity of air and colour, heaven seemed for a moment all around. But there was Cripp, on the boards, sick as a toad. The night behind him? The day to come? But sick all the same.

Joe Reed and J.J. walk around the mullet swim.

Joe looks out on the same scene twenty minutes later.

Done for, body and spirit, and I dropped him off into a shack on the marsh head and he crept into the darkest shadows.

I got to Cripp's Island. It had been overwhelmed by a summer storm a month before and the seas had swamped. A winter flash pool had been filled and a shoal of mullet, a hundred or so strong, had become trapped there and remained safe. Too far above the tideline for the seals, unknown by the netters, they swam their acre of fertile water. I sat and watched. It was like a tench-fishing problem – preoccupied fish gone on daphnia. Here was an explosion of organisms produced by months of strong sun on a shallow salt pan and I did not feel very confident, even though there were big mullet out there. They moved in groups of a dozen or so fish, flashing in the sunlight. One jumped. It was like a trout lake in the desert.

I carried a sackful of baits and put them to fish after fish. A hundred times, a fish was attracted, followed a bait down and left it on the bottom. I tried all the shoals I could see and always the reaction was the same. The sun was well up and the glare on the water grew and forced a general movement into the western corner, which was ribboned with seaweeds. There lay a deeper hole, a rod's length out, and I buried into the sand by it. I threw in handfuls of maggots and layed one on, on an 18 under a red quill. Even though the fish all looked five pounds, what would I not do for a bite? Mullet were around: sometimes the float stirred or lifted; sometimes a patch of sand mushroomed close. I began to hear my heart beat.

There was no shade. No breeze. Already there was a heat haze over the landmass two miles off. Through the glasses, I could pick up the hut, but not Cripp. The sandflies never left me alone. Somehow, the crickets had recolonised after the flood. A lonely bumble-bee droned blindly past out over the sea. Seals were fishing in the surf. There was a tanker on the horizon.

It was 9 a.m. on Cripp's Island when it all happened. The float that had been there, wasn't. The rod that had been in the rests, wasn't. Lying in the sand, the reel was giving line fast to a fish of searing pace. In his leaps, he looked like a sea trout; on his tail walk, he could have been a barracuda; but he had nowhere really to run but round this silly pool. I sloshed to dry land with him safe netted. He weighed 6 lb 5 oz and he went back well.

Happy endings? It seemed so. Cripp was alive in his hut and we were back in harbour as the hotel bar opened and Johnny set them up. Cripp got down the aisle, but he left her half a year later. The pool dried up in the next six weeks and though I managed to save a few fish the rest were food for the gulls.

WIGEON'S SUMMER

A fine house, with cottages and estates, has recently been sold in this area. Latterly, it had run down a lot, hence a low price, though the park, the shoots and the lake were still keepered and kept up. If it had heydays, since the great days, then they took place in the summer of 19—, when an American film director pronounced the entire location to be the ideal setting for his new masterpiece.

The usual fortune was spent – on the roof, the windows, doors, state rooms, the greenhouses, the vegetable garden, the lawns and hedgerows; even the boat-house was rethatched. When all the workmen had gone, just in time for the summer shooting, the actors arrived by trains and cars and even in helicopters on the open meadow by the plantation, so I am told.

Now, the story demanded that the male Star should speak in a broad country dialect and should look and act like the tenant farmers of old, and to school the Star in such ways, Wigeon – worm digger, thatcher, man of all trades – was brought in.

The Star and Wigeon took to each other at once and for the whole of the first morning they sat diligently in the refurbished study learning their 'thars' and their 'thines' until Wigeon suggested that the Jolly Farmers would help their confidence and loosen up their tongues. On their not-very-early return, the two passed the lake and the Star's eyes shone – not for many years had he fished. The States, the South of France, sets and starlets had all contrived to keep him from the real waterside. Wigeon's eyes shone: for just as many years he had wanted in vain to fish this most private, well-keepered lake. In fact, the eyes of the Star and the Wigeon shone together and by mid-afternoon the study was abandoned, tackle was got together and the pair sat contentedly learning their lessons over two dubious rods, quill floats and a crate of brown ale.

The season was not yet quite in, but US dollars brought peace of mind to the owner and the two had exactly one week's fishing that neither would ever forget. It was a week of glorious weather, beautiful parkland, pigeons that cooed day long and tench that bit and fought like greedy schoolboys.

Strange, the two had so much in common, the same hopes and fears, but above all the pleasure in just sitting fishing. It is odd how just to sit there, watching a float weave around, can take all cares off your mind – if there are no records to beat or weights to match. It was just a week of fishing for fun. Not for years, apart from on a set in Berlin, had the Star been up before dawn, and it was rare for Wigeon to keep away from the

The bravest of fish – the tench.

Farmers at lunch time. The two just sat and talked and fished. The Star learnt his 'come you in, bors', his 'nexter morns', his 'rum uns' his 'took queers', forgot to shave, lost all hint of anti-perspirant, knife creased trousers and polished shoes and, the week up, the director decided that he would do. Filming would start and Wigeon was sidelined.

There were three highlights left for him, though, that summer. One day, down by the lake, the Star's leading lady was to be filmed rowing across from the island to the boathouse. Not surprisingly at her first try she capsized, but was saved by Wigeon swimming like a seal and diving like a duck. The incident happened over his favourite tench mark and he told the crew then and there that it would be named Miss C.'s Hole. Respect, and liking for the pun, made him just as quickly change it to Miss C.'s Swim. She kissed him firmly on the mouth – and he got pondweed on his beard.

As a reward, Wigeon was given a line in the Cricket Match scene. When the Star hit a towering six, Wigeon had to shout 'Good shot, bor' into one of the cameras. Twice he got the wrong camera and once he forgot his lines, but he made it at last, and the Star clapped him on the back, saying softly, 'Good lad, Widge'.

Then, right at the end of the shooting, the Star and Wigeon had their last session on the lake. Right till September the weather had held, and the Star had forsaken the farewell party to be after tench, and to be with Wigeon. Together they sat quietly as the dusk fell and the lights from the hall began to fall on the still water. It was a mild night with the bats working busily and the tench throwing up long trails of bubbles around the swim. As it got darker, they rigged up a stage light with a half-mile of cable to illuminate the floats and they carried on catching till the stars were well out and midnight approached.

Before one, Miss C. found them with chicken and champagne, said 'It's lovely here', and sat with them for a while. But she realised that tenchfishers are really happier on their own and she left them with a kiss each.

'You know, Widge, she is right. It is lovely here. I'm going to miss it one hell of a lot.'

'And me,' replied Wigeon. 'And me.'

They stopped till dawn. A much colder dawn now, and the Star caught and held the last tench. There is nothing better than fishing with a friend. He let it go and a shower of leaves followed it into the lake. The two men filled the champagne bottles with water and sank them after it. They took their gear down and shortly afterwards a car arrived to take the Star to Gatwick.

As I said, the place was sold recently – a local solicitor bought it for an anonymous buyer, and the postmistress tells me that Wigeon had a telegram two days after the auction. It read: 'I'm wanting a waterkeeper, bor. The cottage is yours if you want it.'

I expect to see a wisp of smoke from the chimney there before long. Certainly before June, don't you think?

STORY OF A NORFOLK FARM

My long friendship with the farm was never better than tonight. The last fish from the mere was a dream, with the full moon riding high over the house brushed by fleeing silver clouds. A light from the bedroom window reflected off the still water, twice broken by the back of a rolling fish. When the bobbin went away and I struck, the tightening line quivered silver all the way down to the carp. I had to break ice round the margins to meet her and, so cold it was, re-break it to return her. Then I just sat in the utter silence and relived the old times on the estate. The bright night lit up the meadows and woods, the flintworked cottages and Dutch-gabled farmhouse. I could see spires of churches, towers of halls and the dazzle of freezing lakes.

Three summers I worked on the estate from 7 a.m. till 9 p.m., on the potato machine. An hour for lunch, though, when I unhooked the tractor to take me back to the farm to catch a carp with my sandwiches. Back in 1970 it was that I claim to have been the first man to use sweetcorn for carp. Joe, the underkeeper, had given me a pheasant to eat and as I sat on a bale of straw watching my float I found a few undigested grains in the bird's crop. They caught me three carp before the foreman bellowed me from across the fields.

In the Tartar's Head on Friday lunch time over pay packets, pints of mild and flat-cap talk a man told me it was he who had stocked the pond with wildies, back in 1947. Just six he put in, but what a miracle they turned out to be. The pond is less than an acre in area and never deeper than twenty inches. In 1950 it was polluted, it froze solid in 1963 and it drained nearly empty in 1976, but the carp survived, bred and flourished. They share this puddle of water with roach, eels and ducks of all shapes, colours and parentage, and food has become pretty tight indeed. Herein lies the eternal dilemma of these poor tormented fish. For years they have not wanted my baits, but needed them; have suspected them but have

A place that hardly seemed to have changed for decades.

been forced into taking them. Of course, being carp, they are tightly enough wrapped to have perfected defence systems. Now they can take a bait so fast, the bobbin can go up-down, up-down and up again before Wyatt Earp's finger could even twitch.

Of course, as a specimen hunter, I have tried to outwit them. I've freelined, used very long tails, very short tails, soldered the bomb to the hookshank itself, used a size 22 buried in a grain of corn and gone down to 1-pound line. I've used different baits, fished at dusk, dawn and night and now I'm proud to say I hit one bite in eight.

The real answer, as I have found tonight, is to fish in winter. They obviously never have enough food to be able to afford the luxury of hibernation but in temperatures below freezing their metabolism slows them down enough for me to hit them. Being half doped with cold they don't fight much – excepting Nelson. He was the one fish stocked in 1947 with distinguishing marks – just one eye and half one gill cover gone. I got him in 1970 at five pounds but the six times since, including tonight, he's slimmed a bit and seems to be freewheeling at about three and a quarter.

Hector had no time for the carp; he baked one, grilled another,

A view of Marsh Lake – the famous water on the estate.

casseroled a third and then gave up. Eels were his fancy and sometimes he would fish with me over lunch, catch some roach and keep the smallest half dozen in a net. At knock-off, he would kill them and put them on night lines and in the morning he would have at least two big eels to eat. I mention Hector for three reasons. First, he had fished for eels regularly for forty years and I think he knew about them. Second, he always laid his night lines in the stream leading off from the pond, never in the main water itself, which only contained smaller eels. Third, you notice he always used freshly killed deadbaits, because he swore that the eels would not take baits that were even fractionally off, and he proved that to me on several occasions. Having seen this, I wonder if the trend for prebaiting with hedgehog guts and other nasties actually repels the eels. Hector is in his grave now, but I'm sure he'd find the idea most amusing.

During that summer, I met Joe, one of the underkeepers, who showed me the tench water that has since become lusted after by every specimen hunter in the country. When Joe and I first walked through the wicket gate and meadows to that lovely peaceful lake I never knew it would become the Marsh – the breaker of hearts, of friendships, of specimen

All night, sometimes, the lapwings call on the stubble fields.

groups – nor ever guessed at the famous wellies that would push round its banks.

In those days it was fished by very few – Joe and a few locals who came up on bikes. I certainly never caught a lot and was plagued by hordes of tiny rudd and perch, but late in the year I made an effort and dragged out a swim near the boat-house.

I arrived at dawn, which would give me three hours before work, and I caught one male tench of 4 lb 3 oz. I fished hard the rest of the year, never had even a five-pounder and never tried again until the mid-seventies, when the place was unearthed in a big way. Then I was amazed at the change within five years. That weed had gone and even though swims needed dragging in 1980 it was nothing like those early days. More dramatic was the total absence of small fish, but most startling was the size of the tench. Many were catching fish after fish in the five to six pound bracket when in my day they were struggling to make two-thirds of that. If ever proof is needed that tench do grow bigger than formerly, look no further than the Marsh for an example. I just do not believe that the seven-pounders that the Watsons, Plummers and Cliffords have caught there were around in the 1960s.

Those mid-seventies days at the Marsh were interesting ones. I think John Judge was among the first to pioneer the modern trend of tenching at thirty yards plus, using swim feeders and looking for what is now the classic twitch. Very soon the groups moved in and fishing the Marsh was made to appear a specialised business with Crabtree right out of the window. But I always thought the sophistication was out of tune with what is still a straightforward, unsubtle part of the English countryside. I remember a local telling me his girlfriend was 'up the stick' and he was marrying her. Hadn't they taken precautions, I wondered. 'Well, if she couldn't be bothered, didn't see why I should,' he replied. Can you get less ultra-cult than that?

New Directions 1973–1976

I could not date this precisely, but from about 1973 angling seemed to assume an even more central role in my life. Where once it had been important, around this time it dominated. From here on, angling was to become essential to my entire being.

This transformation was confirmed in early 1975 when I moved into a tiny cottage in a small valley village. I shared the place with another fisherman and between us we created for ourselves a universe that existed only around our river, its floodplains and its huge, uncaught fish. At that time fishing even began to smack of something magic. Let me explain. It was as though I sensed new forces at work. I felt that for the first time I had a view into the very nature of life itself. I believed that my awareness was extended so far that it crossed all previous barriers.

I suppose this can be explained by the fact that never before had I spent so much time fishing. Every dawn, every dusk and every nightfall I was there, totally alone, watching the sun rise and set, listening to duck overhead, aware of every sight and sound. The fact that the roach were so large was important too. These great fish that I had wanted so much since the 1950s simply enhanced the dream that I was living. The fact of their size confirmed the fantasy.

Two places on the river were particularly special. Big Bend and the Old Mill. They are so still today. I can never go to either without experiencing a flood of memories and, more important, feelings that have since faded but are easily stirred to life.

Both Big Bend and the Old Mill are majestic riverscapes. Both offer sweeping views over the flat waterland of the Wensum marshes. At both I have caught three-pound roach. Both figure large in the section that follows.

HOLY NIGHT

We are going back many years to a Christmas of magic, to a time that haunts me still. The images of those days are ever fresh and even the music runs in my head now. The music? Oh yes, the music of the river at dusk, of wildfowl on the wind, of ever-lingering organ celebrations to the

When the river runs a dark vein through the whitened fields.

new-born Lord . . . But I am ahead of myself. I must explain.

It was the week before Christmas. I was home in Norfolk from training to be a teacher. I had some money in my pocket, which meant time to spend on any fishing project that excited me. Not surprisingly, as it was in the early days of their boom, it was the Wensum roach that attracted me. Then, as now, these huge fish held great mystery for me and the promise of a week lost on stark lonely floodplains was irresistible.

Wensum roaching was never easy – memory picks out the good times and discards the rest – but I believed I had found a stretch of unlimited potential. Recently, I had witnessed one mammoth fish caught there by a typically lone angler and had seen other monsters topping. Even if the largest fish formed only one shoal, the challenge did not daunt me. After all, to a roach man, the promise could hardly be greater.

Had I have felt any last doubt, then the weather that week would have settled it. Perfect roach conditions do not arrive every winter like this one.

Day after day was rain-freckled and a warm 8° C. The winds were light or fresh, always from the south-west. Never was there a hint of sun and, indeed, sometimes dawn seemed to do little but slightly melt the darkness of the night. There was high pressure due – the forecast said late on Christmas Day – and that, I knew, would make an already difficult task unbearable. It seemed vital therefore to seize the chance that offered itself.

I chose my swim carefully. A kink in the river seemed to give me most of what I wanted. I could see three hundred yards downstream and rather farther up. If a fish should roll in that half-mile, I could be there in minutes. A stand of alder and birch kept some of the wind off the water and created a cocoon of warmth. Finally, the slight bend deepened fractionally from a steady four to five feet. This I felt could encourage roach to stay in the swim after a period of grazing.

So there I decided to sit and set an ambush. Rather than chase my shoal of big roach, I would let them come to me. I was in their area. If I continued to bait, then they would show sooner or later. The walk to the swim was a wild one and to bypass it I moored my dingy on the opposite bank, well up river. Now all I had was a drive down a tiny lane, a short walk and a thirty-second row. Things could not be more simple.

On that far bank, all but facing me, stood a church. It was very ancient with a craggy round Norman tower. There was no village left around it. This I supposed had been a victim of the plague or of sixteenth-century enclosure, when wool kept Norfolk rich and the sheep lords swept even towns away for pasture for their flocks.

For two days then, I was totally alone on the drab plain from before dawn to well after dusk. I felt absorbed into it. Its life became my life. Its damp greens and browns reflected my sodden Barbour, my mud-streaked boots. Mud – there was mud everywhere. I was a blob of mud in an ocean of the stuff. At night, though, an hour after the quick dusks, I would row across the river and drive off into another world. The big fish, I must add, stayed aloof. I did not catch. Those two days I did not even see them.

On the third morning at about 11 a.m. I was aware of music. I stirred from a half-sleep and looked through the low-lying mists to the church. A light shone from the tower there. I walked towards it, bathed in the growing music. It seemed most wonderful in that place – a stream of organ notes that rippled and danced, as if tossed by the stirring breeze, throwing up a beauty I remembered well and yet could not name.

Nor did I lose the sense of being alone. I had seen no one enter the church and now it was more as though the land itself was playing to me. The harmony between water, land, air and angler seemed to be complete. That night I saw a roach roll forty yards beneath my pitch. Everything was now coming together.

23 December was a day like those before it. The depression still dominated, turning day into only a slightly less black form of night with no other change of temperature or wind speed. Only once was there a fleeting smile of sun at mid-morning, hinting that the cloud was less thick, that a new order of weather was on its way. I wanted success and I needed to have it quickly.

Hardly had the fogs and mists settled around the sun once more when the music played again. If anything, on this second day, I found it even more beautiful. Round and round my memory the notes rejoiced. I had to know their name.

I poled over the water, walked the gravel path to the church door and went into the small building. It was a cold, twilit place and only the candles guttering in my draught showed any life at all. I moved down the aisle to the tower and to the organ loft. The music grew in volume until I was bathed in it. Crude and bare the centuries old church was, but then, to me, it was a fabulous temple.

A voice called 'Hello' from the dim recess.

'I'm sorry,' I replied. 'I didn't wish to disturb you, but the music is fascinating me. I recognise the tune so well and yet your adaptation has quite made me forget its name.'

A lady appeared. 'Silent Night,' she said.

'Of course. I used to sing that as a child.'

'I know,' she said. I looked startled.

'All children do, don't they?' she added.

That night roach rolled all around my swim. Sometimes a back came clear, sometimes a dorsal fin and sometimes a tail, big, broad and red, slapped the water only feet from my rod tip. The sound of these fish too was music and for a while their ripples were a continuous swell into the reed frond before me.

They disappeared. They had gone down – to feed, surely – and for an hour my heart beat loud like the pendulum of an old clock. I was so close that even after a blank hour I could not believe that they had left. After two hours, though, I upped rod rests and rowed across the water.

Leaving troubled me greatly. Even as I was doing it, I swore that if need be the next day I would stay on till midnight. I would fish until either I or the weather broke.

Christmas Eve morning at eleven once more, the same lady walked the graveyard and called to me across the river, 'Any luck?'

I shook my head. 'Not a fish yet.'

'You will have soon,' she said, 'you deserve your Christmas present too!'

We both laughed. It was pleasant to share this river world and at times in this, her third rehearsal, I sang snatches of the carol where they fitted her playing. Morning long I remembered midnight services on Christmas Eves in childhood, when I stood between my parents, all of us singing, happy and content.

The roach – the perfect symmetry.

That late afternoon, I could not deny that the low pressure was in shreds. There was an ever-freshening wind and long breaks in the cloud that let in a deep rose sunset. Soon there were stars in widening strands and it grew much, much colder. The mist of drizzle was replaced by pearls of dew but I had resolved to stay on and there was no thought of my giving up.

How quiet it was that silent night. All was calm. All was bright - for now, around 10 p.m., the moon began to shine, and, five hours after sunset, the roach shoal moved once more. Under the new silver light, I saw more of the fish; their heads, their depth, their very scales were highlighted with startling clarity. I felt a sense of inevitability. Now I knew our paths were destined to cross. I watched the dough bobbin with absolute certainty of success.

The church service began across the river from me. Only half aware of the carols, my eyes flitted like a hawk's from bobbin to rod tip and back again. Whenever the wind rose to stir either of them, then my heart all but died within me. And when, at last, the bobbin hit the butt in a gentle sweep upwards, I hesitated dangerously long before laying into the strike.

First the roach plugged away down deep, but as it neared the net it threw the water high in diamond cascades. It shook its great head and, right at the net rim, I saw the silver hook sparkle. By a sliver of skin that roach was mine.

It was huge. It glowed. It absolutely shone like the gold presented to the Lord in his stable. The quest was completed.

I poled across the river that last time. The small congregation was leaving and the organ was playing 'Silent Night' as a farewell. It, like me, was triumphant.

I went into the church and down to the organ loft. The music stopped as the bell chimed midnight and, when all was silent at last, the lady appeared. She looked at my face, so wild with joy in the candlelight, and said, 'Happy Christmas - and how big was it then?'

OPENING DAYS

Of all my opening days, June 1976 will always be dear to me. J.J., Joe Reed and I gathered at Felbrigg, or at 'L.F.' as it was then code-named. Before it became famous, there were no paths to the lake or even around it. Nor were there any swims cut or any other signs of anglers, but there were record rudd there if I had the luck, or the skill, to catch them.

Norfolk June – month of tench and rudd.

Tuesday 15 June had seen a depression track east and by the early evening it had grown cool, wet and windy for us. On the dam wall, the long grass was sodden and spilled seed on our thigh-boots as we cleared a space for the three of us. We put up our gear, mixed and threw out groundbait and waited in the teeth of the bleak weather that came at us down the lake from the north.

Tom, the keeper, made his last round and we talked together under the thick oak tree that kept something of the rain away. Jester, his golden Labrador, was sodden but caught a mole, chased a squirrel and was very happy indeed.

By 9 p.m. it was gloomy and a dreary half-light filled the valley. A tench porpoised ten yards out, so gently, so silently, so swiftly he seemed like a spirit. At 10 the darkness was complete, and the rudd began to roll before us, over our bait. First we heard their splashes, and then as we concentrated we saw their shapes crash out of the waves, head and shoulders upright, resting on their tails an instant and then toppling back into the dark water. To hold them with us at the dam, we fed in tiny balls of bait laced with maggots and corn and prayed for the sixteenth to fall.

Twenty seconds after midnight, my bobbin jerked and fell back into the grass. The fish was a good one. I knew by the sullen way it hugged bottom that it was a rudd of two pounds or more. It wallowed five yards out and as it began to drift onto its side Joe's silver paper reached the butt. He struck and as he did so J.J. was reaching to hit his first bite. By 12.03 all our three rods were hooped over the dam.

We coped with remarkable sanity and by 12.05 three golden rudd lay on the nets in our torchlight. The brilliance of their colours shone back at us. Never have I seen anywhere fish as vivid as those Felbrigg rudd. No words could ever do them justice: they were simply miracles of creation.

At 12.07 I took another. It, too, was large and Joe netted it surely. For two minutes all was quiet until the shoal wheeled back over and chaos struck once more – 12.10 and J.J. was into a fish; 12.11 and so was I; and at 12.12 so, too, was Joe.

At ten yards range, the three big fish were doing what they liked with us. Joe and I tangled our lines and both fish splashed chaotically together. J.J. knocked the groundbait bucket over the dam wall. The torch beams whirled round and round in crazy circles, frightening birds in the treetops and ducks out of the reeds down the lake. A savage gust of wind ripped the umbrella somewhere into the hedgerow, where it struggled, tearing itself against the thorns.

We only had two landing nets. J.J. lifted out his fish, came back to help Joe and me but not until the third or fourth attempt did we scoop out both our rudd, tied up tight in a ball of nylon, bombs and swivels. All we

A Felbrigg tench of the early seventies is weighed.

could do was unhook the fish, pull for breaks and retackle in the ever-mounting storm. Life had never seemed so bitter-sweet.

J.J. was soon fishing again, waiting for the shoal to regroup and resettle over the groundbait. At 12.20 the eighth fish was hooked, just as I recast into the swim. At 12.21 my flake was taken on the drop. So once more, at 12.23, both landing nets were in use again and two more two-pound rudd were hoisted ashore.

The rain grew heavier. The loaves of bread were soaked and the flake would hardly stay on the hook as we cast. The maggots were swimming in their tins. The now shredded umbrella leaked like a cheese grater. Water had got under our hoods, inside our boots and down our necks. We were shivering with cold.

By 12.35 we had gone twelve minutes without a bite and we found it easy to believe that the shoal had gone. In thirty-five minutes we had taken nine two-pound rudd to 2lb 11oz and we could not wish for anything more than a hot bath and a warm bed.

That night was the climax of our rudd fishing at Felbrigg. During following years the numbers of big fish fell away and as far as I am aware none of the huge fish there were ever caught. Overfishing and the overcrowding of rudd in keepnets all added to the natural mortality rate

The first night's haul.

of the old shoal members. When we found Felbrigg the rudd had flourished in the lake's neglect and, looking back, I realised that we probably had the cream of them that night.

TENCHING IN MAYTIME

When the moon is full, like tonight, and when it is cold and clear with a mist rising off the pond by the house, I think of a special tenching night. It was tench in Maytime then, for John and me, on a land-locked East Anglian water that allowed such things up to a few years back.

That night, we had fished late, long after the sunset had painted the reeds with warm honey right up and down the long lake. The cloudless blue sky burned with the afterglow and we caught more and more tench, which bent our rods like reeds against the deepening velvet-blues above. In that last hour as each fish came to the net, it thrashed the water into drops of molten gold.

Hooked in as the sun beams down.

Stars came out in endless whirls from one horizon to the other and a massive moon slowly rose up out of the marshes. It bathed the lake now in silver and the tench abruptly stopped their feeding. We realised it was cold and retreated for the rest of the night into the old railway wagon. We prepared a meal and ate it as always, by Tilley lamp, sharing a bottle of rich, warm ruby port.

Sleep was shot through and through with dreams of big fish. Sometimes I half awoke, watching the moonbeams through the chinks of the roof and walls and the luminous hands of the alarm clock edging towards dawn. There were hints of paraffin, of damp nets and of oars stowed away still muddy, smells both of comfort and adventure as I drifted back to my tench-riddled sleep.

The morning light glowed lemon and lime-green and the water smoked like a fire. The sun was lost in mists. There was not a sound over all the great flat plain and we realised as we walked to our swims that we crunched in thick frost and left dark trails along the whitened bank.

Our tackle was coated in thin ice and the landing nets were frozen to the grass where we had dropped them after the last of the evening's fish. Even the bread crunched and was hard to put on the hook, so we dampened it to make a paste and cast out into the mist.

The water was as quiet as the world. Not until the sun had pulled itself clear into the sky and the vapours had trailed away into oblivion did the bobbins begin to twitch and quiver. Skylarks started to sing, the lake shone in brilliant light and the frost melted into a dew. It would be a beautiful day.

I connected with my first true bite and the clutch yelped. For the following minutes, the light cut like a diamond through the water, gleaming on the tench that fought in the swim beneath me. Its ebony tail beat the body forward endlessly against the pull of the rod. The entire bulk of the fish pulsated into a sledgehammer power force that drove again and again into the silt or urged on towards the reed stems. Its yellow belly glowed as it turned on its side and shovelled along the lake bed, sending skyward a fizz of bubbles. It stood on its head, thrashed the line with that great tail and shivered the glass wand to its very corks.

John netted the fish for me, but, quickly as we took the pictures, we realised that the fish was losing its shine, its wetness. The air was degrees lower than the water temperature and the tench was losing its body heat fast. It was suffering so we let it back at once, and watched it glide away until the angle of the sun's rays hid it from us.

So that May day passed with plentiful fish, with old friends remet and great laughter under an azure sky and an almost summerlike sun. It was evening when our two cars left the marsh and on the downs we both

Maytime, and the fledglings warble in the sedge.

looked back to the shining water snaking its way to the sea wall. We waved goodbye and drove our different ways home, knowing that tired contentment common to all successful fishermen.

Tonight, I think fondly of those out-of-season tench. They were special fish caught in the company of a dear friend. We never kept them in nets, never landed one advanced in spawn, and I am still inclined to think that we did little harm.

TWO-POUNDER FROM THE DEEP END

Roger and I met at dawn, by the church, and took the track down into the misty valley. It should have been a good time – we had our gear and were heading for one of the last Wensum roach strongholds. Though tired, we were both bright, breezy and optimistic of good fish and, as all roach men know, there is nothing so stirring as a deep, bronze-red fin at sunrise. We joked and laughed on the trek across the floodplain, happy as little boys skipping school.

Roger saw it first. A jib in the distance, by the willow tree that was our goal. A real shiver of cold fear ran through us. Our talk stopped. Our walk hurried into a stumbling run.

Our willow-tree swim had gone.

Over it stood a thirty-foot digger. Its bucket had gouged out the guts of what had been a roach sanctuary for the fifteen years I had known it. The forty-year-old willow was hacked back to a runt of tree. The bend was straightened. The shallows, the pool and the deep hole were now a uniform, bureaucratic four feet deep.

What will happen now we have seen before. All the weed along miles has been removed and, as this is one of the few roach-spawning sites remaining, the fry of 1986 will perish without their cover. That flickering hope for the future has been dealt another blow.

The weed removed was the good weed of the ranunculus family. Now, in its place, in the reduced flow that dredging produces, blanket weed will spread to cloak the river's bed. The gravels and chalk will be smothered. Aquatic insects will find it impossible to recolonise. A vital, living waterway has, within a week, been reduced to sterility.

We walked a while up and down the stretch on a lunar landscape of mud and silt. We suddenly felt weary and returned to the cars and to our beds before sunrise.

At home once more, I could not sleep, but walked the woods watching the day unfold. Memories of the Willow Pool flooded back with the

River at dawn.

morning light. Some thirty two-pound roach had fallen to my rod from that one pool over the years. Most had come at dawn or at dusk, generally on the lead, but a few on the float when the light was strong enough to see. Perch had once been a feature of the swim, but now their comeback would be impossible. The senseless destruction of it all!

My brightest memory of the Willow Pool was the very first day I discovered it, a day that developed into the strangest roach session I have ever known.

About eighteen years ago, I set out over a summer to walk the entire Wensum from Fakenham to Norwich, to mark its hotspots and to obtain permission where I could. It was August before I reached the Willow Pool. The farmer immediately gave me fishing rights when I explained my mission and showed me all along his stretch of river.

We came to the strangest of places. In a clearing stood the relics of what had been a formal riverside garden. At its centre was a swimming pool, quite large but very decrepit. The tiling was cracked and weed-covered. The changing-rooms were sagging but the pool still held water. Murky green water came in from the river when it flooded, the farmer told me. As a result, this rotting, Victorian pool even contained fish life.

The farmer and I parted and I went off to fish the Willow Pool. My bag built up: some dace, three perch, five roach to $1\frac{1}{4}$lb and a jack pike. Things were progressing well until the break of a summer storm. The thunder I did not care for but the violent rain was even worse. I stuck it a few minutes then upped tackle and ran the banks to the shelter of the ancient changing-rooms.

The pantiles that remained offered some protection and I sat on a bench watching the rain on the pool in front of me. The storm seemed endless and, to while away the time, I decided to fish the old swimming pool. I rigged up a float and a plummet and made a few exploratory casts.

At first I was disappointed to find only a couple of feet, but then the further down the pool I tried the deeper the water became. Underneath the remains of the diving-board at the far end I located near on seven feet. Scampering down the pool, I scattered a few maggots there and returned to the changing-rooms. A heavily shotted float cast underarm just made the target. An old flower urn served as a rod rest and I sat back to wait.

Nothing happened for a long while, save a frog legging it around and around the pool looking for a beaching place. I landed him with my net. I found I was sharing my quarters with a family of voles, which, for rent, gladly accepted half a loaf.

The skies began to brighten. The rain was only a freckle on the pool when I made my last cast. I stood up, stretched, and gathered my gear

Reflections on the river.

together for a return to Willow Pool. I said farewell to the voles, rescued the frog a second time and reeled in the float. Down in the deep end, I found I had a fish on! It fought quite well but had few snags to aim for in a tile-lined basin and I netted it without trouble.

It was a roach and just scraped over two pounds. I measured it at nearly fifteen inches and at that length it should have been eight or ten ounces heavier. Its coloration, too, was insipidly pale and I reckoned the pool did not have the food stocks for such a fish. Accordingly, I released it back into its true river home.

I returned to the Willow Pool, took another two-pounder before nightfall and left the floodplain a truly happy man. The drainage department has seen to it that those days have gone.

THE FOURTH FISHERMAN

At the turn of the year, I found a broad bend on the river, quite alone in the wilds. The central channel was deep but it shelved rapidly as the water slowed and where the current broke up into a series of small eddies over hard gravel and sand. I fished there three times in the course of a relatively mild week, with some drizzle and low cloud. I was successful on each occasion with chub to five pounds, roach to around two pounds and several dace to fourteen ounces. There was even a good pike in residence, which had followed some of the hooked fish in very closely, pondering whether to strike or not.

On a Friday evening, as I left the bend, I felt very happy with it indeed. I knew it held the promise of even larger fish and, above all, it was my swim alone. As far as I could tell, I was the only person to know of the existence of this hideaway amongst the marshland and the alder-tree scrubland.

I also noticed that the wind had changed and the low mist clouds had cleared away from the east. The stars were bright and a crackling of frost had skimmed the ditches and the standing pools around the cattle troughs.

Later in the night still, as I walked the dog, clouds had formed and when I locked the barn and the sheds a light powdery snow began to fall through the darkness. That decided me to fish the next day only at dusk and to reset the alarm clock from an hour before dawn to a more civilised time. The thought of a Saturday-morning breakfast appealed greatly and I settled to dream of my bend in the river, dark between its white-dusted banks.

The snow lay deep – but fatally marked.

The following afternoon, I started out again over the marshes – brilliant, dazzling acres now under a blue sky and a clear sun. I mused that it was too cold for roach, but I still fancied the day for dace, and as I made my careful way over the last plank bridge I knew that I would not be disappointed.

At the top of the fifty-yard bend, I swung off my gear and made up a float rod, planning to drag a bait slowly along the crease between the main flow and the slacker eddies in the bend. The water ran about four feet deep here, so I set the float a few inches over depth and, all prepared, crept into position amongst the dead sedges along the water-line.

But there, to my shock, were footprints and the marks of a tackle bag and chair, and the ice crust of snow was holed where a rod rest had been plunged through. There was the clear outline of a landing net in the snow and frozen water lay in the imprint. The net had been used. I was dismayed. I felt betrayed. My bend was not mine alone.

I walked the bank, slowly, in thought. What chance of fish had I today, I wondered, if the swim had been disturbed only hours before? The drive, the walk had both been wasted and my head hung low. So it was that my eyes followed even more tracks in the snow.

These, though, were bird marks, about three inches long with three skinny front claws and a long one behind, the so-called first toe. I knew it.

A heron had been there too, wading in the shallows, creating further havoc in the swim. The first fisherman there that day – I was not even the second, but the third. The swim, I knew, would be useless.

Only ten yards below me, the snow had been greatly disturbed, thrown about even, but still in places the marks of yet another intruder were plain. Paw marks this time, with the five toes of the pad joined by a web making in all an impression two or three inches long and much the same broad. I was not even the third fisherman. There had been an otter before me too.

The tracks led, as I feared they would do, to the remains of a fish. It had been a good roach, perhaps even two pounds, now stripped clean from head to tail, with its scales scattered silver on white.

Quite miserable now, I dragged back to my tackle and sat there a while. A heron, a successful otter and a successful angler had all been in my very swim, and it had only been light for six hours. Miraculously, a dace topped five yards beneath me, and another lower down. With no real heart, I squeezed a pinch of flake onto the hook and swung out into the current. Two rod-lengths away, the float tripped out of line and, with a wiggle, disappeared. The rod lugged over into a big roach, my best from the swim.

The afternoon drew into dusk. The full moon came up early and its light off the snow was great enough for me to continue fishing, with the float, into the night. The valley was bleached in a silvery light, strong enough to throw shadows as strong as those before the noon sun, and though the temperatures fell below freezing fish continued to feed. Never had I taken such a bag, and, even though I returned them straight to the river as I caught them, the shoal did not disperse.

I did hear a heron cry from the alder wood opposite me at dusk, probably because he was more angry than I had been to find the bend being used: I did have my supper waiting at home. I never saw the otter, only more tracks, and the other angler I have never met. The snow tell-tales did me no harm, only good, showing me how selfish I had been.

Good fortune is meant to be shared, right down to the fourth fisherman.

DAYS OF THE KESTREL

That first summer evening seems like a fairy tale, the dead roach like a fable of my mind. Now it is hard to believe that golden valley ever existed, or the fish. I lifted her out of the water down there by the island and she

Daylong the kestrel overlooked the valley.

filled my hands. She had not been dead long; her scales blazed in the setting sun, the fins still soft and vivid. The round bite out of her breast still bled a little on my fingers; spawn trickled on my hand. In the wake of the otter there must be roach left, perhaps greater than this massive sister.

Now like legions of grey sheep the clouds come rolling in from the west. For days they have been passing overhead and away down the wide valley. I feel as if I have been here all my life, seen all history, all time in this sombre land by the slow river. From the earliest dawns to the last lights of sundowns hardly any human life have I seen: a tractor on the farthest hillside inching its way across the dark earth, but never the driver; the dogs of the farmer, the shot of the gun, but never a sight of the farmer himself. I sit alone below the hall on the northern ridge where its spires reach into the sky and no one lives. It was burnt and partly destroyed years ago.

At night I sleep still seeing this world. It has become a part of me.

And all the other part is obsessed by the legend of the roach, the biggest Wensum roach. I can see it roll on the darkening water as night seeps in, feel it pull down my rod in a quivering arch, and watch its swirls as I release it back into the cold bay. It is all as magical as the rainbow that came out over me and the hill, even though the sun hardly dipped under the clouds nor was there rain in the air.

All the beauty is magical too. The way the gentle river is rippled by the swans coming round the great bend. Nine of them, proud on the stream, their feathers glinting white against the iron water and dead sedge of the banks. When I first came there were ten, but that last one lies on the marsh with fox-prints all around and its lightest feathers blowing away to the east.

The afternoons grow cold as the invisible sun sets down behind the dykes. Now they come, the soft cries of the barn owls, floating like music on the wind from the long wood and the old cattlesheds. Some lucky nights I have seen one, even the pair, great dappled snowflakes in the sky, or hanging like frozen mist over the long grass.

Now the herons know me they do not move far as I return in the cold light. But the vast flock of Canada geese always rise up and away in a draping curtain over the plain. They go away up the river and it is some time before the cries and the leaden beat of their wings die in the wind. One of these dawns a grebe was there on the water, alone in the winter light, erect on the grey water.

And over all this, day after day, ruled the kestrel cock. On the branches of the dead trees, on the charred spires of the hall, silhouetted on the upland ridge, or hovering and wheeling slowly over the plain, the prince was in his kingdom. Set on fire in a dive to earth past the sun, his plumage glowed deep red. Always silent, always beautiful, whenever I looked over the river, the plains and the marshes. I saw him as constant to this place as the wind.

On that last afternoon he flew, though the wind had turned to the east and snow blew across the sky. He made his last flight over the island, the ducks were coming in home, the fox padded towards the farmyard – and the miracle came!

After all these motionless weeks, the float went, the thumping rod startled me from my dreams and a true fish wallowed beneath me. I felt the heaviness of the net and the cold water on my hands as the snowflakes fell. My scales rose to three pounds five ounces and then relaxed a little and I thought it was not yet my magical fish.

The wind died, the sky grew light and the whole world turned deep copper. The barn owls were more gold than silver and the old hall gleamed in the dusk and suddenly I realised it was my dream fish. The kestrel passed overhead, to the long wood, and I took down my rod and left the wide river.

WAYS OF THE OTTER

The late evening died and a bar of sunlight hit the nursery wall, slowly darkening and fading. The hill outside was just a silhouette against the western sky, and the first stars were appearing.

A small table lamp clicked off, my mother put down the book and her footsteps grew soft down the long passage. Outside a fox barked, another answered, and a summer insect flew against the window pane. Further away, the other side of the wood, the sound of the weirpool just carried through the still insect-humming air and all night my sleep boiled with the foaming white water and the evil, grinning sea-stoats that lived there.

It was three or four years ago, in a brief spell of frost and snow. There is an upland where you can stand and look three miles down the Wensum; see its bends, the splashed pits, the straggling copses and the dark dykes. That day the winter sun was high, the fields looked silver beneath it and the river dark blue. Slowly my binoculars scanned north to south, east to west, and saw nothing – no birds in the air or on the water, no animals in the frozen fields, just two black dots on the water where the river widened and moved into a great slow bend. But they were moving quickly, north against the flow of the water. They left the river. I had to

The ways of the otters – along the river valleys, through the millpools by night.

focus and re-focus quickly as they rippled across the snow-dappled field. Into the dyke, through the tunnel they went and were lost in the dazzling wind-chopped water of the gravel pit.

Overnight the moon sank in cloud, temperatures rose and steady rain had melted the snow by morning when I went down to the pit. In the soft mud around the banks there were otter marks in profusion, and the trail of two animals leading off down the stream on the southern shore. So dark I almost overlooked it, quite as black as the bank on which it lay, was a bream. The rain had kept it fresh and moist to touch. Its fins were still soft, the eyes liquid. Out of its belly was a single bite – a chance whimsical snap of teeth that had ended twenty years of life. As I buried the big fish the rain hardened and grew cold and wiped away the last of the paw prints from the ground.

This year they returned.

On a very light night in February when the moon was almost full and the river looked like a great silver snake beneath it, when the owls hooted early and grew still, when a deep thick frost descended from the very stars, they came again. Numb with the seeping cold, I had lain for hours on the dark bank waiting for the great blue-sided roach to find their way into the deep bend before me. Ten o'clock, and the ice hardened on the rod rings when the otter rose from the water. Dark at first, and then streaked with silver as the moon caught the trickling water on his fur, the brightness of his eyes and the gleaming ivory of his teeth.

His eyes glittered right at me, yet for a second he rose erect, then vanished in a boil of black and silver water. In his dive he fouled my line and the rod clattered off its rests. It jerked and then came free. For five minutes the night was still, then a sharp call upstream, a quick answer and two dark shapes were swimming across the straight towards the ditch that would lead them by dawn to the Blackwater.

The next night I fished, though it was still cold. I took one roach and from its back a bite of flesh had been taken, so deep the bones showed through. The blood trickled darkly in the moonlight and sadly I killed it before fungus set in, leading to inevitable slow and painful death.

Now it is late April. I got up at dawn this morning because my window faces east and the sun woke me early. I walked down the river and across the misty meadow, climbed the stile and the bank to the reed-fringed pit. Then I watched: the kingfisher, the two white grebes and, because the sun was bright enough to give light, yet not so high as to cause reflection on the water, fish. A shoal of rudd came past the gravel spit, rolling at fallen flies; but the carp was not there. I had seen it first on a damp, misty afternoon in late October. I did not know it was a carp then – I just saw a big dark fish moving powerfully away under the water towards the island out in the gloomy lake.

Again the following day I saw it, lying black against the sandbars. This time I was so close I could see the great scattered scales on its back. At night came a frost and soon the easterly gales, and the fish went away into the pool's deepest gullies to spend the long winter.

Now, I expected to see it again. I looked all along the sandbars for it, out across the surface for the bulging ripples as it surfaced, and in the deeper holes for the smokescreen of bubbles and debris as it churned through the mud. But there was nothing but the white grebes diving.

My attention was caught by a red squirrel playing in the long grass on the margin of the pit. The grasses tapered away onto a shingle bank whitened by the drought. On it lay a carcass, as large as a young seal. Her eyes had been eaten by the crows, rats had tugged and ripped at her flesh, but she had died of the two otter bites in the throat and neck. A great carp – not the biggest that has ever lived in East Anglia, but dwarfing any caught. Ten, twenty, perhaps even thirty years she had swum the pools. I eased a scale off her back and like a golden plate it lay, filling my hands with the sun, the rising sun that reminded me of the sunset so long ago, when my mother read to me and when the carp before me was just one of a million fry.

And I thought of those words again: 'We disdain to eat them all; we just bite out their soft throats and suck their sweet juice – oh, so good!'

Even if I could I would never kill the otters for what they do. Though it is wicked, it is no worse than the way man is slowly destroying the Norfolk bequeathed to him. And for ten thousand years otter and man have been hunting on Anglia's watercourses. And for longer than that otters have wandered over the land, travelling from river mouth to watershed, from one river to another, down immemorial paths along streams and salt marshes, resting where long-dead generations of their ancestors have passed. On every otter's trail, in every pad's print lies the image of man's past and future, his dependence upon nature and his cruelty and savagery towards it.

TWO MEN FISHING FOR ROACH

Before I start to talk about its roach, I would like you to imagine the character of the river – or at least the stretch with the fish. It is very, very beautiful. It is deep for an East Anglian river, with depths to eleven feet. Also it is wide, sometimes thirty yards. Finally, it is a long stretch, four miles between two mills, all gradually deepening and widening to the bottom sluices.

And it is all but unfished; the water looks so barren, and to an extent it is. There are very few fish, just here and there, with hundreds of empty yards between. But what roach they are – few under two pounds eight ounces, and most two pounds ten ounces or above.

6 January was a dull, wet day with very strong westerly winds. But it was warm, and at three in the afternoon the water temperature was 44°F. For five days I had been feeding in bread steadily, morning and evening, and only then did I feel ready to try. Until four o'clock I was plagued by the squally wind that played havoc with my swinging ping-pong bobbin.

I was ready to move home when across the dark water I saw a fox. For twenty minutes it stayed, grubbing on the bank, snouting about for water rats, voles, dabchicks or wild ducks coming in with the dusk. So at twenty-past four I decided to stay for the last of the light. And just before five o'clock the bobbin dropped, a fraction only, but quickly enough to be interesting. The rod just bent and bent as I picked it up. Then it kicked, and without a wriggle a roach came to the net. She weighed two pounds and fifteen ounces.

Not surprisingly, for the last sixty-six days of the season John Judge and I fished the area hard with only one short break for the February freeze-up. Otherwise we fished every night from four o'clock to eight thirty-ish, and many early mornings. In about five hundred rod hours we had another thirteen fish – see what I mean about the fish being few! But they were big – the smallest was a 'freak' of 2lb 1oz, the largest 3lb 2oz and the rest averaged 2lb 12½oz. More important, I think we gained some insight into the behaviour of very big roach.

Never before had I fished so sustainedly in just one relatively small swim. Week after week on a bend about forty yards long with a ten-foot-wide, eleven-foot-deep channel running like a spine through it. I feel I knew more about the fish then than any I had hunted before because of the short distance between us. I was sitting often only five yards from my bait and every breath upon it registered. At night, I was so close that I could see roach bubbles break or hear the tip of a dorsal fin flick the water.

Strangely, they selected their feeding places at isolated spots along the channel. Strange, because at that depth the current is negligible. Bread, line, everything is pulled until it sinks six feet down while for the next five feet the descent is vertical through virtually slack water. All the channel is gravel and clean, there are no attractive snags or obstructions. But there are two slight saucer depressions just off it, one three yards long and two yards wide, the other slightly less – and the bites come from here. I had to get the cast just right in the darkness or I would not get a flicker. I do not know why now, when all the bottom is equally dark and slow.

But after well over a hundred trips some feeding patterns are taking shape. Most obviously, of the twenty-eight bites we saw, only two came in the daylight; and, even in the half-light of dusk, only another four. All the rest have come well into the night, most of them ninety minutes after true darkness has set in.

Within reason, whatever the temperature or the wind, the current or the water colour, this, with these big fish at that time, was a reliable pattern. These big fish were true nocturnal feeders. I had expected to catch fish at dawn but in twenty sessions I had just one bite and that the merest flicker. I noticed, as with bream, that nights of the full moon were the least likely to produce. It seemed that any light was harmful and we went with most hope in the darkest nights.

Throughout, we took regular temperature checks. John Wilson queried our faith in fishing the deepest swims. We answered that for protection and for food build-up the fish would go there. We hoped too that the stiller water and lower light would attract them. What we found, though, was that these holes were warmer and lost their warmth more slowly in a cold wind or frost: whereas the margins and even swims three or four feet deep soon dropped from 43° to 38° or 39° in a rising wind, the stiller deep swims kept around 41°F. Owen Wentworth said recently that below 45°F the chance of roach was slim. Here we found that anything over 38° or 39° gave us a chance. But in these conditions we found we had to wait longer for bites - often over two hours into darkness - and then they might be the briefest of bites and easily missable. Something I cannot understand is that on these freezing nights big fish often rolled.

The temperature affected the nature as well as the number of bites. There were several types we experienced: twitch drops and lifts and drop and lift humdingers. And they were all problems. The drop or lift of the bobbin was the easiest - the roach basically either moved away or towards you. The other divisions were more complicated. A twitch perhaps can mean that a fish has flicked the line, nosed the bait, or has sucked it in and is lying still, chewing it. On some twitches I struck and there was nothing and on others the roach would be deeply hooked. Again, others I left only for the bobbin to go swinging away thirty seconds later, probably as the fish felt the hard hook in its throat and bolted. On reflection, I think it is right to strike if the twitch either up or down is anything above an inch - less and I am inclined to leave it.

The jerky bites that travel a few inches I love because I do not often miss them. We feel the fish has just picked up the bait and is moving slowly away with it, taking it deeper. Mostly, such bites mean a well hooked fish.

A lot more difficult are the humdingers, when the bobbin either rises or drops very quickly indeed. Most of these are missed. Some perhaps are line bites; perhaps some are bream bites. One night in March I am sure two came from an otter fishing the channel and catching the line. Perhaps the rest came from roach, suspicious and bolting, possibly already caught or pricked and frightened by the familiar drag (though this does not explain why we always missed them).

Two more interesting things about bites. I had a far greater percentage of missed bites in the early night than later, when a hooked fish became more common. Perhaps the confidence of the big fish increases as the light fades.

Second, it seemed that flake has to be in the swim for at least twenty minutes before the take. By then the bait has lost any definite shape and softened to merge, all formless, with the bottom. Probably, as ground-bait samples are thrown in long before the fish come on the feed, this is how they recognise and accept it.

By now you realise two things: we used flake for bait and legered it. We

Simple, basic creatures, but suspicious and easily scared.

felt flake had several advantages over maggots. From the safety point of view we were able to use heavier tackle with it – size 8 to 10 hooks and three- or four-pound line. We felt that if we used bigger hooks with more maggots on there was a danger of a maggot bending over the point and deflecting the strike. We believed, as a second reason, that flake is better seen at night. Maggots are small and can burrow. Neither do they smell enough to compensate for this. Also we preferred to prebait with bread, feeling that there was less chance of eels or small fish moving in. And steady prebaiting we found to be important. These big fish appear sensitive to a rhythm. Constant feeding once, perhaps twice a day, and the swim builds up and up.

Bread could become the basis of their winter diet: they become accustomed to the splash of bread lumps hitting the surface, perhaps even attracted by it. It did seem that big roach are creatures of habit, unlikely to be opportunist feeders, rather looking for a regular, reliable food source. Certainly, once we had weaned them to it, it could be hard not to deep-hook them on some bites.

To leger seemed obvious to us. A float would have been more affected by the wind or surface weed. Also it would be more difficult to keep a float still enough in even a slack flow for the bait to remain motionless. Judge tried quivertipping on three occasions but, like me, he reverted to the link leger and bobbin set-up.

On 22 January the wind blew from the south-west. There was a slight drizzle in the air, the water temperature was 43° F and I was fishing by a quarter to five in the afternoon expecting bites. Twenty-past five and the first, a drop! I missed it and was rattled. Quarter to six, the second – twitch up, pause, up again. Strike! A whine of the clutch! A break-off above the hook! Shaking now so badly, it took me until ten to six to retackle. Twenty-three minutes past six and a steady run towards the butt ring. Heavy resistance – something big, deep, going fast. No! The line fluttered back.

For a while this was a nightmare. Fishing close in to avoid as much as possible the effect of current and wind we ran the constant hazard of breaks on such large fish in deep water. We tackled the problem in different ways. Judge took a light ten-foot rod, a flexible Avon type with a test curve of twelve ounces or so. I pondered the switch to a soft-actioned rod of the Persuader type, but stuck (through financial necessity) to the thirteen-footer. Simply, I slackened the clutch until it gave at the slightest pressure and struck steadily and gently.

One of the wildest river valleys.

Neither of us would ever claim we mastered the roach of even this short stretch – nature is too perverse for that. Probably things will be different next winter even here. If I can just have conveyed the excitement I am content.

'Got down to the farm at three thirty. Saw the old boy again. Talked about the same thing. Baited John's swim – I'm glad I don't have to fish it – exposed. Down to my swim. I've decided to throw in mash as well as flake. There may come a time when they associate flake with pain ... It seems a bit warmer today, wind's as strong though, gustier perhaps. The bobbin jumped and I missed hitting that by a mile. Daydreaming. Leave it for fifteen minutes or so. Nothing. Recast. Down and across. Nothing. Recast straight out. Middle of run (I hope). Very difficult to see now. Must be about a quarter past five. Bang! Bobbin shoots up. Drops down. I strike. Clutch screams. Silence. Nothing. Line snapped. Weak as hell. S——t! New line! S——t! S——t! S——t!' (John Judge's diary, 21 Jan 1976).

The Last Decade 1977–1987

In some ways, this period began badly. There had crept into the specialist angling scene an unpleasantness and a vindictiveness that marred the whole spirit of the sport. For once, the competitiveness of many was directed not against the fish but against fellow anglers. Friendships were broken. Feuds were struck. The fishing press and the angling grapevine carried rumour and lies, often both snide and dirty. I was as bad as many and most were as bad as I. There are many of us who fished in the mid-1970s who behaved on occasion like spoiled children.

This tarnished phase I have touched on in the first two articles of the final section. Angling, however, recovered and has moved on closer to the true spirit of the sport. Though there still is some unpleasantness – there always has been and there always will be in any sport – the majority of fishermen have recognised problems far greater than their own personal egos and sensitivities.

Since 1975, angling has come under increasing pressure from many sources. Agricultural practices have had adverse effects on rivers everywhere as chemical run-off and land drainage have increased. Water authorities continue to dredge rivers in short-sighted, ill informed ways. Line, litter and lead shot have combined to ruin our reputation with the general public. The serious fisherman has seen these developments and realised that to set his face against his angling brothers now is madness.

The work done by the Pike Anglers' Club, the National Association of Specialist Anglers, the Anglers' Co-operative Association and the various carp societies has done much to forge a new unity in recent years. Our love for the environment must now be mirrored by the effort to work for its preservation.

The period saw more anglers travel for their sport and, though the bulk of my fishing remained Norfolk-based, I too have fished every part of the British Isles. I have widened the scope of my quests to include barbel, salmon, catfish and even golden orfe. In the ten years past, I have been everywhere and fished for everything in British freshwaters. So has the richness of angling grown for me. Nor has its fascination faded a minnow's length.

THE WIZARD POSTPONED

There is a branch of literature called the fantastic. It aims at the imagination, often by using everyday situations, but put in a surprising way. It has been described as the impossible seeping into the possible. Its purpose: not quite to explain things, but to be enjoyable and to lead us to view things afresh, to think anew.

One of the earliest writers of fantastic literature was the fourteenth-century author Don Juan Manuel. Of royal blood, a tyrant, a prototype for Machiavelli, brutal to his three wives, he ordered a monastery to be built to guard his manuscripts – documents which came to light in the 1930s. One of his plots I have borrowed, but have converted it into a fishing tale that should have some meaning. I have left the original title for those curious enough to want to seek it out.

In the city of Dorwich there was a young man, a student, who had a burning desire to master the art of catching big fish. He heard that a certain man, D'Arcy, had more skill in the field than anyone else, so he, Grover the student, went in search of the master.

D'Arcy was reading in his great study when Grover called and was let in by the manservant. He was received most cordially; a drink was poured

There was a strange estate . . .

for him, a seat was pulled up to the fire, for it was late autumn and cold outside. Grover told of his search, of his desire to know good waters, find killing baits and methods, and catch monster fish. D'Arcy nodded his head and said that Grover should be told all, and begged that Grover should stay for a supper of pheasant shot in the woods there around his house.

D'Arcy called to the cook to prepare the birds and then led Grover out of the house, across the leaf-strewn lawns, over a bridge spanning a wonderful lake where carp were leaping, to a marble folly at the edge of the forest.

Inside, Grover stumbled in the darkness, felt the dampness on the walls which seeped into the air itself. He was relieved when the lamp flickered on to a treasure-house of maps, charts, prints and photographs. Everywhere lay rod sections, dismantled reels, and complicated hooking rigs. In the corner, saucepans were simmering. Over all hung the rich luxuriant smell of oriental essences, herbs and spices.

D'Arcy lifted up a huge trunk and laid it open on the table. Inside were diaries, recipes – everything from a lifetime's study. Grover was made to promise that he would remember D'Arcy, give him due credit for his catches to come, and remain true to him and all his secrets.

'Yes, yes,' cried Grover, 'I will always keep faith with you. Please let us now begin. Tell me all, please, now.'

The session of secret sharing began. It lasted and lasted. Time passed. The afternoon outside darkened into night. Rain beat against the windows. The wind howled down the chimney stacks. Bats flew in the black dome above them and the rats began to squeak and scuffle for the offcast baits.

Dogs barked in the distance, outside a wild cat began to howl. Voices by the window, fists banged on the door. Two men burst into the room; the sleet glistened in their beards.

'Grover, Grover, man, you're in the syndicate. You're in, man. Come with us now to meet Mintram.'

Grover wept with joy at the news. Five years he had waited for the syndicate place. 'I am pleased my house should witness such joy,' spoke up D'Arcy. 'But, please, just remember your promise to me.'

'Of course, dear man. Always I will,' replied Grover, but even as he was leaving the seeds of forgetfulness were being sown.

Grover's catches were great that following season. Before the next one, D'Arcy wrote reminding Grover of his promises. Would he take D'Arcy to the syndicate water? No, no. It wasn't possible yet. Perhaps next year. You know how clannish specimen groups are. Not my fault. And so on ...

Seasons went by. Each time D'Arcy wrote, Grover replied in an unsatisfactory way. D'Arcy grew old. His fortunes faded. Grover grew more famous. He wrote for magazines, he knew the heroes, but he was called the greatest. His picture was on the bedroom walls of star-struck boys and he rarely came to fish the paltry water around Dorwich. However, years on he heard of a roach boom – no, a tench lake – and returned.

As chance would have it, D'Arcy was by the lake. He was feeble, tired and ill, but still skilful, still determined, and at a great range he hooked a huge tench. Grover was the only angler there and he heard D'Arcy's cries for help, but, as was common in those horrible times, he was full of jealousy for anyone else's captures and he pretended not to hear. The tench escaped.

D'Arcy had been bivvying for days. He had grown too weak to move and called across the lake for Grover to bring him food. Grover got to his feet, strolled around the water and spat at the old man. 'You fool, you dotard. Beg. Beg, beg for years. I owe you nothing.'

D'Arcy could only reply that he would leave, but asked again for food before the journey. Once more Grover refused him, whereupon D'Arcy, whose face had changed in a strange fashion, more youthful and strong, stood up erect and said in a true, firm voice: 'In that case I will eat the pheasants that I ordered for tonight.'

The cook came forward with the roasted birds and at once Grover found himself back in the stone room by the forest and lake in the late autumn, no more than an unknown, laughed at on all big-fish waters. He stuttered his excuses, but D'Arcy said that the test was sufficient, and with that same great courtesy led him without food or knowledge to the gates of his estate and bade him farewell.

THE SCENE

A recent article, 'Wild Guesses and Wicked Lies', which described deception in the specimen fish world, had in it more than an echo from the past, from the bad old days of the 1970s when, I believe, big-fish angling ethics sank to an all-time low.

In that era specimen hunters discovered that there were nowhere nearly so many big fish around as we had once believed. The 'repeat capture syndrome' revealed that most waters held only a few outsize fish and that stocks were not limitless. At the same time, we saw the obvious decline in many rivers and estate lakes, and the feeling grew that there were fewer big fish than there were anglers in pursuit of them.

The result was a progressive fall in angling standards and morals in many areas. Squabbles seemed to proliferate. Friendships were broken. Lies and rumours were spread north, south, east and west and nobody was above attack.

In fact the more successful an angler was the more jealousy he attracted and the greater became the backbiting that followed his journeys. I say 'journeys' because the 1970s saw the lift-off of the circuit angler – the man who would fish Oxfordshire one weekend, Norfolk the next and Lomond the third.

Of course, the more these men travelled and the greater their catches became, so did the reputations, the pressures and the hassles grow. It was the boom time of name dropping, of star gazing, and it came to many as a shock to find that even the media heroes got into tangles, made bad casts and swore when they missed a bite.

Specialist tackle really took off. Rods had to start 'looking right' – this was as important as the job they did. 'You can tell an angler', it was written, 'by his set-up'! So it became as vital to mount the rods at the right angle as to get the bait in the right place. You could blank all season, but yet still *look* the part. It was this easy to become an 'instant' specimen hunter, almost without ever having had a bite!

Big-fish waters had always been nicknamed – for example, Twitchalot Pool and even Redmire from years back – but in the seventies this grew quite topsy-turvy, totally out of hand. There was T.C., the Marsh, the Lagoon, the Willows, Rotten Bodies and on and on in an endless list. One of my roach waters even became Extremely Unmentionable, shortened to EMU for convenience and even further secrecy.

Photographs were vetted for any tell-tale sign. Lovely shots never made it in the press, because there was a particular oak tree in the background, or the chimney of a keeper's cottage protruded over the captor's left shoulder.

Equally stupid, it seems now, were all the false location reports that went in during those days. Men tied themselves in more knots than the proverbial eel. Norfolk is a perfect example. Take the scenario: a man catches a good roach from the Wensum and reports it from the Bure; the week following he actually catches a bigger roach from the Bure and reports that from the Yare. After a good session on the Yare he says the two-pounders from there came from the Waveney and, of course, all along everybody believed they were Wensum fish anyway.

Some anglers went to endless trouble to 'spot' the famous. Stories grew that there were in existence lists of the car registrations of the successful. Certainly one of my acquaintances was followed one Saturday

Modernity – buzzers, bobbins and rests all in perfect symmetry.

dawn as he set out towards the Kennet. (I believe it was the Kennet, though he might not have told even me the truth!) My acquaintance drove around the the city, town and countryside for two full hours with his 'shadow' in hot pursuit. Finally, he pulled back into his own drive and went indoors to a startled wife and breakfast.

There were other, dirtier tricks played. A favourite was to drop evil-smelling soap in some quantity into a man's prebaited swim. You can guess how many fish he caught from that area again. Much more unpleasant were the sinister tricks played on the fish themselves. I do not think that the claiming of false weights was much practised, but worse was. It was the heyday of the 'big bag' shot and certainly large numbers of big fish were netted or sacked for hours or even days to make an impressive show at the end. Mercifully, that kind of ego trip is now past: no one thinks it is praiseworthy any longer to see fish with tattered scales, split fins or bloodied lips.

All these things I hope are behind us, firmly locked in a bygone age.

THE MASTER PLAN

The master plan is dreamt up in the armchair and put into practice at the waterside. It is the satisfying fusion of intellectual imagination and hard physical graft. When it works it is beautiful, but why are my master plans almost always cock-ups? In five trips to Awe after *Salmo ferox*, I've hooked eight perch and two thermoclines; whilst after walking more miles in the Fens than I care to think about, I've yet to catch a pike there the equal of my best tench. But with one master plan I did have a degree of success – perhaps because it was not mine alone.

The lake is totally isolated, private, some thirty acres in extent and completely surrounded by woodland. We made contact with the farmer who grudgingly allowed us to fish. The banks, he pointed out, were everywhere marsh and his boat would be an absolute necessity. He left us at the head of a narrow path and we cut our way through thick alders as far as the boat-house. Some time last century the boat must have been a good one; now bailing was as important as rowing. But John steered us out of the dyke on to the main body of the water.

The water was as clear as a Scottish river so we could see every detail of the bottom. Weed growth was negligible and for a while all we saw were eels snaking away from us to burrow in the silt. We both stood up to act as human sails and the breeze drifted us down the lake. When we reached the end we rowed back to begin another glide.

We saw nothing and realised that any fish present were seeing us bearing down and were leaving fast, so we anchored and waited for them to come to us. We saw several shoals of bream, all small in number, but big fish. The biggest group comprised eight fish, all seven pounds plus. The shoals were very mobile, moving quickly in midwater. Often there were bow-waves in the shallows, and frequently the glimpse of a bronze back or fin. Most interesting was a shoal of five fish that circled the boat for some time. These five bream looked absolutely jet-black. Not dark brown, but black as coal.

The lake shelved from nine feet at the west end to two in the easternmost bay. At one place the bed rose steeply from seven foot up to four foot in an abrupt ledge. Nowhere could we fish from the bank, the farmer was right about that, and, as the boat meant suicide, a platform was essential. We decided to build it opposite the ledge where we had a choice of deep or shallow swims. The area was well lilied – that helped give the right atmosphere.

Building that platform so far from civilisation was a nightmare. Each trip to the site with materials meant a very long drive, a 35-minute walk through the swamps at the height of the mosquito season, and then a 25-minute row to the ledge with the boat settling lower in the water all the time.

We assembled a sledgehammer, one pound of five-inch nails and one pound of three-inch nails. For wood, we collected planks for the floor and the project provided me with the incentive to unscrew the grotesque door that had blighted our bathroom for ages. Support poles and crossbeams we knew we could cut from the alders and ashes on site on the marsh itself.

It was two hours' work to select four ash trees for the platform legs. We wanted them straight, at least three inches in diameter and eight feet long to give both strength and stability. The ends were sawn into points and sledgehammered six feet into the bank. More ash trunks provided the crossbeams to be jointed to the supports. To give the structure strength, four five-inch nails were driven at 45° angles through the crossbeam into each support, and then hammered upwards to curl round it and cradle it.

A lovely fish – a worthwhile end to the quest.

The planks and the bathroom door then went on the structure, fastened to the crossbeams by the three-inch nails. Frequent testings by the 12½-stone Nunn took place and suspect planks were discarded. Finally, jagged or protruding wood was sawn away and the fringe of reeds between the stage and the water was made good again and the stage was ready. It measured about thirteen foot by seven foot and wasn't half bad, we felt, for woodwork class rejects. In fact, apart from a scissor rack, it was the only thing I'd ever really made.

Conventional heavy groundbaiting was not a favourite if only because of the physical discomfort of carrying weights through the swamp. Apart from this, we have done less well with stodge on clear waters and we doubted if there were enough bream to eat large amounts of bait. The massive amount of eels made us reluctant to use maggots, casters, brandlings or even anything based on trout pellets. From the start we used mixtures of sweetcorn, hemp, rice, sultanas and different beans, which were scattered in the area from the boat on the way to the staging. We strayed from normal bream groundbait practice by putting it in sparsely over a wide area, rather than in a small heavy concentration. One reason for this is that with small mobile groups of fish there might be more chance of them seeing bait over a wide area. Secondly, when the bream are feeding 'on the move', they get the bait well within their mouths and give bites which are easier to hit.

The first night I had three bream: 8 lb 1 oz, 7 lb 6 oz and 7 lb 5 oz. I lost a big one that kited to my left and made the lily beds. I got one tench of just under six pounds on sweetcorn, but all the bream came on flake. It is common, I find, with bream, roach and rudd that though they eat the groundbait particles readily, flake hookbait gets fish more regularly.

We used the staging frequently and found that on clear nights which cooled quickly the bream moved into the deep water and over our baits by late dusk. On muggy, overcast evenings, they stayed in the shallow bays much longer and bites might not come till well after midnight.

We never did land a black bream and I began to think it was a trick of the light on the water and that the shoal was no darker than the rest. Later, though, in conversation with one of the farmer's men, we mentioned the matter. He himself had seen a black bream in the rushes, dead after spawning. Some bream in the upper Bure twenty years ago were reputedly black, so perhaps the strain really does exist. I can only think they must be very beautiful fish, especially if, as the farm labourer stated, they have red fins to boot. I would like to think that this season we will get one so that this master plan might be fully satisfied. That would certainly make a change.

THURNE PIKE – A COMIC CON? DECEMBER 1982

Up until mid-December, I had spent twelve sessions on the Hickling, Heigham Sound, River Thurne complex, dazzled by the piking potential, preparing for a Christmas assault, when I could go hell for leather after a fish somewhere in the thirty region. All the evidence I had collected seemed to suggest that a majority of pike had followed the food fish off the open shallow broads into the deeper River Thurne. In the pre-Christmas period big catches of bream had been taken in the Martham area, whilst roach had moved lower down around Potter Heigham. Furthermore, the Thurne seemed a more intimate companion than the vast unsheltered acres of Hickling; Heigham–Horsey is closed until February, and the river would be less likely to freeze over and thwart me in a cold snap.

I adopted, therefore, an old, time-tested specimen hunter's approach. I was sure that the pike I wanted were somewhere in the two and a half

Looking up into the wastes of Heigham Sound, with Hickling beyond.

miles of the upper Thurne between Potter Bridge and Somerton Broad. I would concentrate there – taking in Candle Dyke and the southern tip of the sound – until I had read the place, and located and caught fish. It never seemed easy, but certainly very possible.

To publish an angling diary is nothing new, but here I think it is valid. These extracts come from a book that has been a constant companion, carried snug in the Barbour pocket but well herring-stained by now. The frozen-fingered writing has often been illegible and I have done the editing that seemed necessary. Nearly all days I fished dawn till dusk, for example, and I ran the whole gamut of methods and baits – excepting livebaits.

16 December 1982

Strong/gale winds. Clear with occasional cloud. 5–7°C. Very heavy flood tide that did not run till after 2 p.m. Water everywhere – in and out of the chalets, across the paths. Leap-frogged from High's Mill past a couple of other pike anglers along to Candle Dyke corner. Nil.

17 December

Dying wind to force 3. Very clear. 3–6°C. Another strong flood tide. Fished from High's Mill almost to Martham Ferry in bright sun that set the reeds on fire. The sky was a summer seaside blue and the tops of the windmills looked white as ice cream cones. Cormorants constantly overhead – but none stopped over. I do wonder if these high salt tides are pushing fish about. Fished hard with drifting and static deadbaits.

On rod 2 trotted sprats on light gear amidst constant groundbaiting. Threw off an oil slick some hundred yards long and attracted almost too many gulls to continue.

19 December

Gale/storm force wind. Intermittent heavy rain. 6–8°C. Fished with Nick Beardmore. Walked the north bank to Candle Dyke corner. Impossible to fish with that south-westerly in your face. Back at the Ferry Basin a big pike had been seen swirling. That and the knowledge that roach were in evidence made us stop. Fished four rods with selection of baits for nothing but extreme cold. Dave Phillips appeared out of the storm and was quite rightly proud of his own 'upper Thurne Pike' taken some time before. 9lbs 2oz only – but a Thurne pike.

20 December

Strong south-westerly. Bright, 4–6°C. Moored in the mouth of Candle Dyke away from the wind. A little after midday a cormorant struggled into the face of the wind and settled on the river. It dived four times and came up with a bream of around a pound. Ate it and was away over the marsh. This is an event. I have found fodder fish. Pike cannot be far.

21 December

Dropping westerly. Breaking cloud to give clear spells. Temps 5–7°C. Considering the flood tide, walked along the north bank from Potter to be able to fish the sheltered corner of Candle Dyke. Very confident. Dominic came with me to wield the cameras and talk. Fished hard with statics, drifting and twitched baits. Sent sprat rubby dubbies down the flood into the corner eddy. Nil. In the late afternoon walked up Candle Dyke to the old eel set and fished in a still golden sunset with the rushes glowing all the way up into the sound. A pair of marsh harriers were working the meadow ditches. It was a fine sight.

22 December

Bright, stiffening westerly. 5°C. White cumulus piled like snow peaks over the sea. The sheds of Heigham Holme vivid in the sunlight. In the afternoon trolled with John Nunn from Brown's Boatyard, up Candle Dyke and all around Heigham Sound itself. Duck everywhere. The two harriers with us a while. No fish. No signs. No anglers. Just the blue sky and the sugar-mountain skies. Stopped off at Candle Dyke corner until nightfall with birds crossing the quarter moon all the way to the Hickling roost. Nil.

23 December

Very cold and bright. Spun baits around the Potter basins most of the day. Nil. Nothing to be said.

24 December

Thaw in the night. Brisk westerly. Drizzle. 7°C. Worked hard around Candle Dyke corner and up to the ferry at Martham, all along the north bank. Met a man who took a big twenty a while back. Since then he has had blanks and reckons to have lost the fodder fish – and the pike. As the afternoon progressed I worked towards the sound. The wind slackened, temperatures rose and in the bays where the warm air came in, mists began to rise. It is a chilling place this, in the wintertime. Nil.

25–27 December

I only fished once. It was a case of concessions to humankind – and of lying low, licking wounds and thinking. After Christmas I decided to spend time again upon the mile up river of Martham Ferry to Dungeon Corner. I had fished it intensively in the preparation run-up for nothing – but the place had feel. Still weedy, sheltered – and the word was out that bream were hanging around the influx from Stubbs Mill.

I defrosted my small stock of eel, trout, roach and bream – all summer pleasure angler victims – as an alternative to seabaits. I pondered more on the old 'pike by moonlight' theory. Denis Pye wrote about it and there are those who still swear by it. Perhaps it is a chain reaction – the pike being activated by the bream shoals' beginning to feed. And the week following would be one of the full moon.

I became increasingly intrigued by the pike pack idea, which I still see

Without a boat, no man can start on Broadland.

as a type of highly mobile hotspot. In a huge complex of this type the pike now behave like roaming bedouins, living when and where they can. Always, I believed, just around the next reedbed would be my nirvana and a haul of pike to make everything worth while.

At other times over Christmas I became depressed, felt stupid in continuing, realising that in twenty-one trips I had not caught, or even seen caught, or even seen, one pike. And yet, had not I heard of a string of fish caught along the river during my time on it: three at 3lb and one each at 7lb, 7½lb, 9lb 2oz, 11lb, 11½lb, 14lb 2oz, 17lb 14oz, 24lb, 25½lb, 27lb 12oz, and 33lb?

28 December

Slight overnight frost. Bright, fresh westerly. 5–7°C. By lunch I had worked up to Dungeon Corner and there miles into nowhere chanced into two London pikers. They, like I, had nothing and were just wondering if the whole thing were a 'comic con'. I could offer little to reassure them and perhaps this is the real value of this account - to paint in the realities behind the newspaper sensations. Back at the Ferry after dark met Chris Turnbull's friend Jimmy, who had taken a three-pounder up river. Something of note!

29 December

Bright. Calm. 8–9°C. Began at Potter spinning roach around the bridge, the boat basins and the chalets. Worked up the south bank. Nil. Then up the north bank, stopping off everywhere up to Candle Dyke corner. About four, a boat came down off the Broads and the two guys seemed interested in me. I stuck it out well into the night for nothing and then had a hard hike home past the eel set and over the marsh.

30 December

Mild, overcast - perfect weather and I hit the Dungeon region with all I had got. At four I reeled in the rods, threw in the baits, and with them the towel. Goodbye Thurne. Good riddance to the whole blasted place.

Here on New Year's Day, I can only think of conclusions. I hope that I have not stepped on anyone's toes by publishing so exact and true an account of the attempt, though I cannot see this leading to anything but an exodus from the entire area. Perhaps the reports of big fish have been in part a hoax; perhaps I have made mistakes; perhaps my refusal to livebait, or the result of the rather high salt tides of the pre-Christmas days, have denied me fish. Possibly some of you are laughing over the clues I missed or the stones I left unturned. If so, the best of luck to you, for you won't see me back on the Thurne this winter.

And, if I have a final word to say, it is that the Hickling–Thurne complex does indeed hold very large pike – but they are very, very thin on the ground.

AUTHOR'S NOTE

What I wrote in 1982 is interesting in hindsight of the dramatic events since. Obviously, the Hickling–Thurne complex has produced two forty-pound-plus pike since then and a string of further thirties to boot. Also, the killer algae prymnesium, which flourishes in brackish water, has hit in several succeeding summers, killing even more big pike and thinning out these fine predators even further. I have no doubt very big fish still exist in ones and twos in these lost acres, but the angling pressure, so intense from 1983 to 1985, is now largely off. Trout reservoirs now offer a more realistic chance of every piker's dream – the forty. This is good. Believe me, this much-abused region needs every breathing space it can snatch.

Since 1982, I have modified my views on livebaiting. Then, I did not do it and this cost me fish. Now, I am less squeamish and realise that pike are so fickle that not to livebait is to tie at least one hand behind the back. I would resist all present attempts to make the practice illegal. To ban livebaiting would reduce the number of pike men and weaken angling further. Also, if we admit that livebaiting is unnecessarily cruel, then it is a short step to conceding that *all* our fishing is unacceptable.

I do agree that livebaiting practices should be made as humane as is possible and that we should only take bait fish from environments that will genuinely not miss their presence. I would also urge fish farms to produce disease-free baits for pikers, to further lessen the drain on natural waters.

But a ban? Never! Whilst there are so many attacks made on the waterside environment it needs every angler there is to defend it. And, compared with the widespread abuses that mankind inflicts on the animal kingdom, livebaiting is but a pinprick. Let us first prohibit poultry farms, intensive cattle and sheep breeding, pig units and the horrors of deep sea fishing and *then* let us look at livebaiting again.

As a footnote, the two Londoners I met in the wilds on 28 December of that year were none other than Eddie Turner and Bill Hancock – two of the most adventurous pikers around in the 1980s. Hardly had I left them when Eddy took a thirty-pounder from the Thurne.

A fisherman's life!

THE RECORD ORFE HUNT

The story so far: in 1980 I got to know of the existence of two lakes, each about one acre, which held nothing at all but a stock of golden orfe. They were, in fact, dams in a well wooded valley little used or visited other than for duck flighting. From what I could gather the orfe had been put in years back.

I estimated the lower dam to contain in the region of a hundred fish from perhaps ½lb to 2lb. The upper dam, however, was quite different. There the original fish had not spawned, but grown to a massive size. I hesitated to put a weight to them. I would only go as far as to say that they were five pounds plus. But here comes the rub: there were only four remaining. Four fish in an acre or more of water.

I spent my days last summer watching the fish, big and small, getting to know them, preparing for if and when I got permission to fish. The orfe spent all the daylight hours patrolling their lakes. They used no particular routes, and cruised at steady speeds six inches or so subsurface. Every ten or fifteen minutes they just hung and rested and then after a minute moved off once more. Strangely, I never saw one fish, large or small, take any food whatsoever. This did not worry me in the least, then: I felt that like bream or tench they had specific nocturnal or dawn feeding spells.

Later in the year, I got the permission that I so wanted. I began to lay my plans for the summer of 1981.

Part one of the hunt was delayed by a thick algal bloom. Keith, my partner in the attempt, and the man who had set the whole thing up, and I raked swims but saw nothing at all. Reluctantly, we delayed fishing till the water should clear. With just four fish in the lake some sight of them was vital.

In the first week of July the bloom went quite suddenly and dramatically, virtually overnight in fact. Early one morning I got to the top of the hill and looked down on a crystal lake and on four great orange torpedoes gently circuiting it at an old man's walking pace. I went to see Keith; now we were in business.

It came about that I could organise eight nearly full days on the lake

Big fish often milling at my feet – but uncatchable.

and between us we assembled six rods, tench-type with four-pound line, several pounds of sweet corn and bread. The bank was cleared at a corner of the dam and from there our rods could fan out to cover at least half of the patrol routes. Two pounds of corn was scattered in a long arc and the hooked grains followed. Bobbins went on and virtually in shifts we sat it out through over sixty beautiful but actionless hours. It made me think of normally stocked waters where the bobbins are always twitching or dragging and you put the movements down to drift or wind or weed. But here, though there was wind and weed and drift, the bobbins did absolutely nothing.

Then, at 11 p.m. on the third night, they did – until midnight they tremored and shook with frequent $\frac{1}{4}$–$\frac{1}{2}$ inch sharp lifts. Most I left and nothing developed; some I struck at with no contact at all. After an hour the movements ceased and the rest of the night was totally quiet. That fourth day Keith was afraid that the corn was probably uneaten and was beginning to sour the area, so I pushed out over the area in a boat. Most of the corn was still there, three feet down, and we immediately revised our plans.

The fourth, fifth, and sixth days we moved to a swim on the dam itself where we could fish close in, over deeper water. We began to use a greater variety of baits – concentrating on maggots, but alternating with bread, brandlings, caterpillars, moths, and so on. All to no avail.

On the seventh day I tried conventional fly fishing to the orfe. Each time the shoal came close I put a new pattern to them. The only response was when one turned to look at a Corixa, but it never followed. And on the eighth day I slept in the sun as the fish whiled their lives away.

Away from the lakes, through the rest of July, my defeat irked me more and more. Again I realised that I had still not seen either the big or the little orfe feed. Obviously they did, but when, how and upon what I knew not. Nor could I understand why, having seen so many baits so close, at least one fish had not accepted just out of curiosity. Daphnia in the lakes had something to do with the case, as did their total naivety of man and baits, but I was determined, and in the first two weeks of August was back again with Keith at the dam side.

This time we planned to fish hard at dawn and dusk and to spend the daylight hours stalking the orfe, presenting baits to them, watching them, learning as we went. I also decided to try for the smaller fish, both to boost my confidence and to study them in detail.

By now it was harvest time, with convoys of combines in the Norfolk lanes, and Keith could not fish all he liked. Not that he missed out. Under blue skies the orfe continued to drift and the small fish were no easier than the big ones.

At the end of that first week there was a change in the weather. It came in with mists, then low clouds and rain. By Saturday the dams lay under humid, drizzly skies. Soon after dawn it was apparent that the orfe were in a highly charged mood. Big and little fish were breaking the surface in slow rolls and with heavy splashes. Smaller orfe were taking a hatch of light sedges so avidly that it seemed this was the time I had prayed for. With a self cocker, size 18, and double bronze maggot I cast to the shoal of rising fish. Almost immediately I was into one and witnessed one of the more impressive sights of my career. It fought well and then surfaced in a blaze of colour. Its shoulders were like varnished orange – a colour such as I had never seen or guessed at before, not even on the psychedelic LP covers of the past. I landed three in an hour, up to a pound and a half. All were, in the true sense, fabulous. From the dazzling shoulders the orange melted to salmon-tinged silver around the stomach and, even on that dull morning, they almost literally glittered.

Then, almost with a shock, I realised that these orfe were roach! Or, at least, take their oriental colours away and they were. Shape, fins, eyes, mouth, scales – I checked each feature and but for the flood of colours

John Bailey forlorn on the orfe lake.

there lay three prime roach. I hurried for Keith. We took photographs and hurried to the top dam for the big fish before the feeding spell should finish.

The rest of the day we spent there, and failed. The weather broke back fine again and even the small fish became impossible once more.

Only once have I experienced such problems with species; that was ten years ago with true wild creek mullet. I can truly say I never expected any problems with the orfe but now, writing after twenty-two entirely fruitless days, I am at a loss. My final card is to wait until late September when falling temperatures have put down the food but not yet the fish. I am excited even now: that orfe will outshine the setting autumn sun.

THE VAN MAN

It's 8 p.m. when you decide to go. You know that fishing is for fun, that it is only a part of life, not the whole, and that the travelling circus of angling is a treadmill to be avoided. You know that once you swore to be done with the road and to settle for local-caught fish that mean much irrespective of their size. But the summer is dying on you: it is the last chance before the winter and you have to go.

Half past the hour and I begin to mix the baits. Enough for 300 pieces is measured out and the colour and the taste and the eggs – damn, where are the eggs? – and I am rolling and boiling till the kitchen stinks of pear drops and steam and the hands go the colour of a jaundice sufferer.

By 10 p.m. I move on to get the gear together. Two hundred yards of new Sylcast fill up the spools; I tie up hairs on a dozen Lion d'Or's and re-elasticate a couple of catapults. A quick check – two rods, two reels, four rod rests, two buzzers, hooks, bombs, nets, torches, scales, scissors, baiting needles and cameras. Foam. Foam for line tensioning. Where do I get foam at this time of night? I cut up a cushion for a dozen cubes.

11.30 p.m. and Sharon raids the freezer for victuals and I have provisions for four days if I need them. Now I investigate the drinks cupboard for a Special Brew supply.

Midnight. The van. Oh, God – the van! The dipstick is far too short to reach oil until three pints are delivered and the radiator is low on water too. The tyre pressures, if any, will have to do and I clean the midges, mosquitoes and moths of a hot summer off the screen and the lamps. Not

A fish to travel for.

a Turbo – inside, a turdo – and the litter will stay on, some of it useful sometimes. Cheque book in, cheque card, a tenner or two and, of course, the AA card.

12.15 a.m. An alarm call is ordered, but there is no real need. You know, don't you, that you do not sleep properly with travel and big fish on the mind. It's a warm night, with thunder about a long way off, and I turn repeatedly, throwing off the covers, dreaming strange fantasies until the phone rings – a merciful release.

3.15 a.m. and I am away. The van is alone on the deserted ring road and then I am off south through the lonely Suffolk Chases. Occasional lorries signal me past and the air from the windows sometimes smells of straw burning, and carries the dampness of a typical late-summer heavy dew.

By 4.30 a.m. dawn is a trace in the east, and I am on the motorway. Still no traffic and the van is in her stride. As in the old days when she was young on the M3 to the Avon, or the M5 to the Severn or the M4 to Wilstone, I get her to seventy and think I will be there sooner. An orange light flickers in the grey of the dashboard and I slacken back a pace.

The new town is not stirring at 5 a.m. – just the cats and an urban fox – and at 5.25 I turn down the track to the lake. Dave is asleep behind the wheel but wakes up as I swing in beside him. An instant smile of welcome from him makes the whole journey well worth while already and we agree that the day looks good. It looks at once even better when Dave unloads Sylvia's picnic hamper, which needs us both to carry it to the swim. I think back to her previous feasts – ham salads, quiches, pies. Will it be pâté for tea?

At 5.50 I put out thirty boilies on the fringe of the lilies fifty yards off. Ten minutes later, it is light enough to see my baits hit water over them and I reel the lines in tight, wedge them with foam in the second ring, put on a bobbin, switch off the anti-reverse and sit back until 6.03, when I get fast into a good mid-double mirror. The utter beauty of the fish and the excitement of the whole affair strike me. Only three hours before, I was asleep in a bed four counties away, and now I am living a dawn I used to dream of as a boy cranking to the local fishless lock pool.

Carp came throughout what was a perfect day. I got them off the bottom at distance and as the sun got high I followed them to the shallows and had three big fish on floaters. I had another in the margins and began to feel truly invincible as a carp hunter. The afternoon cooled quickly as it does at the tail end of an Indian summer and the shoals drifted away back to the deeper water. I, of course, followed.

Just before 6 p.m. two big fish come into my patch and at once drop down off the surface. There are at least ten boilies and my hooked ones out there. The bait I know works, and the fish are almost sure to feed. I position the net, check the reel just as it begins to backwind to a quick run. At 6.05 I am into a big carp. You know, don't you, just by the way it goes heavy and determined and then hugs bottom for a rest and there is precious little you can do about it.

At 6.10 it kites towards lilies on my left. I just never know what to do with a quick-moving kiting fish but Dave is a hero, wades in up to his middle to frighten it back into clear water. It fights on the surface, both fish and water golden with the sunset. I net it with a sob of relief as it kicks a spray of shimmering water high over the rushes. It is the mid-twenty I wanted. Dave and I crack a can.

Half-past six and anything else would be an anticlimax. I can be home at 9 p.m. in time for a drink, a meal and a bath and perhaps a call to Chris T. He will be back from Dorset by now with a barbel under his belt and I want to catch him before he goes catfishing in Germany. So, it's into the van, man, with seventy thousand fishing miles on the clock and I don't regret an inch of the way.

THE HUNTING OF MOBY DICK

Times are when something you say or write comes back to haunt you for years. The year was 1975 and a Norfolk angling club the place where I said: 'If I can see a chub in clear water then I will always expect to catch it. However big, however shy, once I have found it I will put it on the bank before long.'

It is 1986 now and Moby Dick has taught me the nonsense of that statement. If ever a fish has shown me never to be arrogant then it must be Moby.

I saw him in July in a well-worn swim above Norwich, known to all who fish hereabouts. That first instant, I took him for a small-to-medium common carp, so great was his width and so large his scales. Only when he turned and rose up through the water did I see him for what he was – an immensely long, deep and broad chub. If ever my six-pounder was saying hello, it was now.

Apart from his size, the only strangeness about the fish was an ivory whiteness to his head and his left flank. I named him Moby Dick on both the counts of hugeness and colour. And, just as that famous whale led its hunter Captain Ahab a merry dance over the seven seas, so was the chub to torment me on the Wensum.

I learnt soon that the fish was a hungry one but that two problems stood in my way. First, he was one of a shoal of thirty lesser specimens.

One of Moby's lesser brothers.

Second, he was clever, a mastermind of the underwater world. I came to learn that if ever a fish should prove capable of thought on a near-human level then that fish would be Moby . . . But, I am ahead of myself. Back we must go to the early days and retrace the steps of that hunt.

A great number of his companions, all hungry as chub ever are, convinced me that it was hopeless to fish blind or at night. Over three days a dozen chub to four pounds proved that. No, Moby had to be stalked. A bait had to be put to him, precisely, individually, if I were going to cheat his smaller neighbours. Fortunately the river was clear and I could see what I was doing. Also there was plentiful cover to use, but there my advantages ended.

I soon found that Moby would leave the cover of his raft and inspect the first bait that was drifted near to him. But once that first cast was refused then all further attempts – even with change baits – were totally ignored. It was as if Moby knew that an angler had moved in and it would pay him to lie low, under his coverlet of green.

Quite obviously my next step was to anchor a bait close to the raft rather than fish it on the move. This is how 95 per cent of Norfolk chub men fish, watching the quiver, and this I am quite sure our Moby knew. Certainly, any static bait left him totally unmoved. I might have legered a lump of rock for all the interest he paid me on the bottom.

So, I came to realise that my first attempt with a moving bait had to be perfect in every way or that session I could wave him goodbye, wish him good day and move down river for a barbel. I began to concentrate on presenting a bait at the right depth, with the right speed of fall, at the same pace as the river and on hook and line that were as inconspicuous as possible. Away from the fish, I tried again and again with bait after bait. Sometimes I used a float and other times I freelined. All combinations of shot were tried until at last I began to feel happy that I had the best combination for that flow rate with both particles and bigger baits.

The next day I moved into the raft swim with confidence high. A big bait was my opening approach – a huge scoop of bread flake moulded around a size 4 hook that would take in water and bounce the gravels under his very nose. It trundled towards him. He cocked an eye, when, dammit, a four-pounder appeared faster than a Polaris, scoffed the lot and put an end to that opening campaign.

Next day, I returned with two pounds of corn and a different plan altogether. For an hour I fed in the loose grains until I turned the water before me into a mass of surging, heaving chub. The threes and fours I had fighting for feed by my bank. Moby kept under the raft opposite,

Watching a float pinned against the far bushes.

coming out now and again when I put two or three yellow grains down his side. Everything was set: the smaller fish busy and lured away; Moby interested and all alone. I felt I was close.

I had changed from conventional line to Drennan double strength 6 lb test. Perfect. A size 14 buried deep in a grain of corn, a number 6 shot six inches up, and a tiny quill at three feet completed the outfit. Now, I would have just the one chance.

An underarm flick and the bait landed dead in line to knock at Moby's very front door. I steered it to him. At four feet, the big chub saw the bait and stiffened. Two feet and he came into open water to watch. A foot now and he came up to intercept. Nine inches, six inches, a nose-length and a confident swallow and Moby was pulling my string like a sperm whale from the tropics.

I lost him. It was keep him from that raft or say goodbye. The line held. The knots took it, but the hook came back straight as a needle. Like the Moby of old, the chub flicked his tail and was gone.

THE FOUR-HOUR CARP CHASE

Always remember that a fish does not have to be huge to present a challenge, to be exciting or to fight well. Even a moderate carp by the outsized standards of Wraysbury, Yateley, Homersfield or Redmire can be the worthy focus of a day.

I got to the water, only a tiny pond, about mid-afternoon. A gusty breeze around the treetops had the effect of blowing all the surface scum and broken-off weed to a corner of the lake where the lilies grow. Further, as this area was itself out of the wind's path and was catching a good deal of sunlight, I felt sure a carp would be there.

And so it was. At thirty yards range, a good fish for the pool began to hump. The sun danced on his back as he wallowed and turned. Sometimes he raised his dorsal fin, languidly, like washing out to dry, and sometimes his tail fin draped over him like a leather sail.

I watched carefully. At approximate ten-minute intervals the fish shook itself, stretched, yawned I guess, and made a small tour of his world. He would paddle a few yards at most and then settle back to drowse against a dislodged clump of yellow flag.

After half an hour, I reckoned I had his behavioural pattern well worked out and I fired a floater to him. It landed too close and he sank a while. When he reappeared, I put a dozen of the baits around the route of his wanderings and waited.

On his first tour, he sucked in three. He took them slowly, carefully, with much bubbling and slurping, as though he wanted them but was not confident and would not be rushed. Each offering he nosed, with his great cream lips searching around and around to check for a line.

Now I went as light as I dared, and cast a floater into his patch. It landed a couple of yards from him and was tethered by a bomb, both to give me casting weight and to hold it in position against the growing wind drift.

An hour passed. Three times the carp gave my bait a hard, long look and went on along his way. This first ruse was not going to work. Indeed, I began to wonder about his catchability at all that day, and, as a fall-back, I began to feed mini-boilies two rods out to pull in any carp cruising close.

I noticed that water was beginning to push slightly left to right where my carp wallowed, and as a result I set up a second rig. A small bubble float would give me weight now and would hold up the line to catch that surface movement. I cast three yards to the carp's left and a little beyond him. I hoped to use that slight current to push the bait right up to him, down his mouth even, if he opened it to have a casual snore.

The ploy began to work. Six minutes after casting, the floater was up to him, just inches away from his head. Through binoculars, I swear I

Satisfaction.

could see his wise old eyes following it. The water began to well. He shifted his bulk around for a take, thought better of it and waddled off for a turn around his beat. When he returned the floater was long gone – four or five feet downwind – and that was the effective end of phase two.

Tall trees reached up to grasp the slowly sinking sun. Crooked shadows hobbled across the pool and that of a giant oak fell over my carp. The evening developed a chill and, sure enough, the fish sank lower, lower and went down altogether. My chance, I was pretty sure, was blown.

I had a sandwich, a beer and a thought or two on the evening to come. The pressure was off now. The intense concentration I had paid that fish eased. I found its legacy was a slight headache and a wonderment that three hours could pass so quickly. My back against an alder tree, I had time to listen to the song of the pigeons and the tapping of the woodpeckers. And little by little, I felt my eyes close.

A very positive slurp awoke me. Almost at my feet a fish approached some stray floaters. It was *my* carp once more! He picked off the last buoyant biscuit, strayed over that carpet of mini-boilies spread hours earlier, hovered and went down.

And, grief, how he guzzled! His pectorals beat the water into a whirl of

Stalking – the essence of small-water carping.

vortices and the silt began to curl up around him like a haze of brown woodsmoke.

He was so close that I decided to float fish – not an indulgent fancy, but a very effective way of taking carp close in. A peacock quill, painted green, was fished on the lift method to a mini-boilie side-hooked on a size 10. Into the cauldron of bubbles I lobbed the lot.

So shallow was the water that as the carp fed, his tail tipped surface. I constantly steered away the float to keep the line from tickling his tummy and scaring him away – knowing exactly where the line falls is another advantage of the float, you see.

And there it was. The float rose, lay flat and zipped under all in a glorious reward for four hours' hard work. Here was my carp at last, pulling steadily off into the pool.

The pigeons, I believe, clapped their wings in applause and, though in the net I knew the carp was no more than a mid-double, he was my target and I was happy. The day had been rich and no man can ask more of his fishing than that.

TENCHFISHER'S DAY

Most were shadows of bronze from copper to mahogany through to black. Some, though, were bottle green and a few appeared almost vermilion. One of the shapes nearly looked the legendary golden that all tenchfishers hunt. Most of the fish could be estimated at two pounds through to four but later some very big tench came in from the deeper water of the lake and looked to be nearer seven, eight or even more.

The monsters did not stop. They passed through the channel to the bare sand-bottomed swim, churned up clouds of silt with their twenty-odd-inch bodies and slid quickly back into dark water.

Late summer England at dawn and a tench lake lay before me, yet, strange to say, I had been disappointed when I awoke. Before, at midnight, the moon had been out and the stars had studded the endless velvet sky but, before morning, cloud had come in from the west and the water reflected drab greens and greys. The wind had risen too, and now it sighed through the massive oak that had been planted back in Tudor times as wood for ships to meet the threat of the Armada from Spain.

Up the lake, the hall looked benevolently on, occasional hints of sun catching its brickwork, winking on the windows and domed turrets. The Friesians grazed over the ocean of pasture and pigeon wings fanned in the warm air.

Noted tenchfisher, Roger Miller, plays . . .

Even the swim was drawn from Sheringham or B.B., cut deep into the reed and yellow flag, loud with the sound of warblers. The hole in the weed was only a rod's length out so there was little advanced tackle around me. I rigged up no long-range feeder, just a quill dropped by some ageing crow and licked with red paint. On the water there it was a sight centuries of anglers would have recognised, some of whom must have fished in this park on this bank and caught the ancestors of these tench of today.

For me to catch, I had to stop those shadows and hold them with me, away from the weed. I steadily fed a hemp-maggot mix, trickling it in when the tench appeared in their ones and twos, hoping they would eventually follow it down and the fun could begin.

It was an hour before a tench upped and head-walked and a puffball of silt and sand ballooned at his lips. A fizz of bubbles hung over him as he righted and moved away, but others were attracted by the activity and began to move in.

... lands ...

... and holds a lovely estate lake fish.

One by one, they tipped and browsed – working the bed with slow, studied concentration. The crow quill stirred and swayed as their flanks and fins caressed the line and lifted the shot, but it never once moved with purpose to a taking fish.

The cloud broke up. Sun burst through. Temperatures soared and the sand on the lake bed glowed. The wind dropped and the lake mirrored the hall, still as a galleon in the doldrums. Like a party down past the dregs, the swim emptied of tench. The morning spell was over.

I slept most of the day out in the shade of a tree. A fitful sleep it was, constantly aware of the damselflies and the bigger dragonflies when they hovered over me on their leaden wings. The casual anglers came, generally failed, and went. Only the small roach took a bashing and a few bootlace eels that did not live to tell the tale. Evening, and the cloud returned on a lively breeze and the last of the picnics was packed away.

Over the shelf came the tench in earnest, back on to the bait, right to the rod tip as though the swim had been in their dreams all day long. Now there was no hesitation. The sand clouded, grew almost muddy and became crazed with bubbles.

All power and paddle fins.

Two fish were hooked, played and landed but their fight only attracted more tench in and persuaded their brethren to feed on even more heavily.

That middling light drew on, when, although it is not dark, the colours have faded and the first owl will call at any second. Bream rolled a hundred yards out. A carp crashed down by the dam – it became an evening you would stake your life upon.

The bats were at work when once again over the shelf the big boys came in. These were shapes two feet long, burly fish burrowing under the same crow quill. The day was coming to its climax. I was an ace from success and my beating heart knew it.

The quill cocks; it moves; it's down. A bow-wave sweeps over the flats and the reel backwinds a thousand times. On he goes, in deep water now, and I'm in there to my knees to keep the pressure on. The moon is looking out on me.

This is the way to end a tenchfisher's day.

AUGUST AT WHITE LILIES POOL

There was a period in early and mid August when the country world seemed to stand on its head. Of course, urban England is aware of hard weather but deep in the country, as an angler, you can never forget it.

The wheat crop was flattened, green and full of rubbish. The combines could not start, or in places were bogged down, or, at best, put in a morning before more wet westerlies blew in. Peas had already been poor and the raspberry crop was on its way to a disaster. Hay drooped uncut on the river meadows and the potatoes were speckled with blight for it had been too damp even to spray. In short, the land was sodden, like a sponge, the texture of a pudding.

The fishing was no better. Day followed day of cold winds, weak, cloud-interrupted sunshine and inch upon inch of deadening rain. It was as if autumn were come early. Carp everywhere moved from the shallows and went down deep under the weeds. Tench melted from catches in lake and pit as the waters cleared out from algal blooms and the daphnia hosts withered. Bream fishing flourished briefly but the heavy winds on open lakes seemed to keep the shoals on constant patrol, never predictable in their feeding or route pattern.

And yet, out of the wind, when the sun shone, it was true August for a while, here and there in sheltered pockets in woods and valleys. It was on such an afternoon when the clouds blew themselves apart that I thought of going to White Lilies.

The sheltering lily beds.

The path through the plantation is a long one. The air was full of that special smell of resin and the pine needles made a thick carpet under my feet. Squirrels played over my head, caught in outline against the blue sky and the high, racing white clouds. Over all was the music of the trees, sighing and whispering in the winds. Surely, White Lilies is a special place, hardly known, yet free to all.

Beneath the crag it lay, with not a ripple wrinkling the pool's surface. There was only a slight swaying of the water and the occasional puffball of thistledown to acknowledge the force five above. Then, as I looked again, a lily pad rose in a gust, but otherwise the place was as it should be on any August day.

The sun beat down on the sheltered sand cliff and lizards stretched out to the heat. Butterflies dotted the air, the pine cones crackled and burst as though in a slow oven and, best of all to me, the big rudd were on the surface, cruising in small shoals twenty yards from the bankside.

In the glowing water they were plainly seen; their fins were that brightest of red, like a cut when the blood first flows. Their scales were truly golden – not an insipid yellow or a coarser bronze, but the real, undebased bright metal. These are the most perfect of fish, stocked a generation ago and never tampered with in the lonely plantation. There

The lake nestles in a valley, well protected by the forest.

is no hint of hybrid to them. If any biologist wanted a rudd sample to set all standards he would come here.

There are twenty or thirty fish and all now wary of me since I caught the first ones as small fish nearly fifteen years ago. Each season since, I have landed a brace or so until every single rudd must have known the feel of a hook. Now, they all weigh from 1¾ pounds and I guess they must be twenty years old.

They are wise, big fish who know all my dodges so the afternoon wore on, and, though loose crusts were taken, baited ones were not, even on 1.1 lb line. Free-falling maggots were sucked in quite happily, but not mine, even on a size 20 hook. Grains of corn were picked off the shelf where the lilies grow, but not mine with the size 16 buried to invisibility.

I contemplated silly things – fly fishing with a carefully presented sedge or hooking up one of the water boatmen so busy on the submerged sandbank. I lay back, very warm now, and a dart of blue hovered and went in, plop, by the lilies. Good news, I thought. The rudd must have spawned to produce the fry now attracting the kingfisher. God willing, I could be hunting rudd at White Lilies for years to come.

The maggots, I noticed, were turning fast in the heat. I already had some sinkers which were taken only a foot under the surface in a

A rudd – one of my most cherished captures.

succession of easy confident swirls. I was in business once again! I skimmed off several floaters and, choosing the largest, I buried a size 16 deep into it. At my feet, I tested its fall rate alongside half a dozen sinkers. The hooked caster went down very slightly faster, I changed to a size 18, and the synchronisation was perfect.

Cast and free offerings were all but simultaneous. The little crystal float landed at the very edge of the sprinkled casters and I held my breath. Four, perhaps five seconds or it would not be taken at all. Over six, and the hooked caster would dangle there, scorned by all, and defeat for the first time would be staring me in the face.

Three seconds and the float zipped under. Mine was not even the last to go! The deception had been absolute. I had had my little piece of August once more down at White Lilies.

OLD STUMPY

I had tried for those fish in the weeks past in the daylight hours, and failed. I fished well into the night and still caught nothing. But I saw them many times, on the surface in boils of gold or amidst the lily roots, shaking the waxed green paddles above them. I had seen them feed too, bubbling from fifteen and sixteen feet down in the algae-bloomed water.

For a week, for a month, for the whole season it began to seem that the big, wise crucians would have all the best of it. Tubs of butter they looked like, barrels of bronze – fattened, I presumed, on blood worm, daphnia and the tiny nameless nymphs of the silted acres.

On an impulse I tried a dawn session. The usual activity was greatly increased. There were more trains of bubbles and more fish showed on the surface than I had witnessed before and sometimes the float even wavered in the growing light. Twice I struck – at air – but the signs seemed to be right. That same night, I set the alarm for 3 a.m., confident in what the coming morning would bring.

Thunder rippled through the heavy air. Lightning shot the clouds in the south. The daytime temperatures had hardly fallen at all. Night insects played outside the bedroom window under the canopy of the chestnut tree and I hardly slept at all. Rain began to fall, in single drops so large they could be heard individually on the leaves, on the gravel and against the window. And then it poured.

The chestnut started to cascade like a forty-foot fountain and the gutters ran awash. Sometimes the room lit up to the storm and the house sparrows scuffled under the tiles as, no doubt, water trickled into the eaves of old dried straw and spider webs. Before the clock could ring, the storm had passed, the night was placid, cool and still. The air was fresh and, if anything, my hopes were higher still. In the dregs of the night, I made off to the lake.

The roads were still streaming from the downpour and in the hollows they were under water. In the estate, the long grasses were sodden and the pathway led to the lake through avenues of dripping beech and oak.

Wood Pool lay still, reflecting the growing gleam in the sky. I tackled up and set down by the alder tree in the corner by the dam. Now, it was light enough to make out the float by the rod tip. A cuckoo began to call and after it the wood pigeons followed from the enveloping parkland. They are the sound of Norfolk's woods and copses and the spirit of summer there. They make a morning for me. I can still hear their song.

A kingfisher began its day, skimming off the fry that dimple for the insects drowned by the storm, and the big common nosed his blunt-headed way along the margins after his breakfast. Already his scales were glowing in the vibrance of the bright morning and the delicate mandarin of his pectorals were quite clear to me. He went down on the shelf and the silt cloud spread before him.

The crucian bubbles were beginning to rise, in lazy strings that lay like small pearls around the float. A fish splashed in a topsy-turvy way and waved his paddle of a dorsal at the world. Still my float lay at half cock, the corn untouched it seemed. Yet, when I reeled in, the grain had gone.

I watched more intently and sure enough from time to time the quill quivered and its angle to the water would alter just a degree or two. The birdsong, the common were forgotten: the battle was on. Again and again I smothered a strike and eased the rod back into the rests. Twice more the corn had been removed by these fish with the stealth of a cat. So on the next shake of the float I went through with the strike and the rod just stopped there, half-way up, bent and drumming to the fish. There is no mistaking the crucian on the hook: the head-jabbing dives, the silt kicking and the fight that is down deep until old stumpy has not got a breath left in his body.

He was a shade under three pounds, but I had found no real answer. He was hooked in the top of the snout, not really tricked at all but just unlucky to be near a flicked hook. And, in a long series of dawns, I never

A rare day when everything went right.

had another. The crucians of the pool are my stumbling block. The story has no real end.

THE BARBEL HUNTER'S WORLD

It was one of the last late afternoons of the season. The day had become mild and, though the rain had died away, it remained overcast. I walked through the acres of reed and sedge and, by four, settled into the bushes swim at the head of the beat.

I sat well back, within the still-living tree. My rod poked through the bare branches that skirted the river. Straight wood against crooked wood. Straight as a ruler still is the James Mark IV Avon and a perfect rod for the job that night.

A red float was top-and-bottomed, well over depth, riding the current easily. The line was seven pounds. The hook was an 8, the strongest in the box. The 42 inch net was up, propped like a great web against the steely sky. I was not after babies here.

The barbel, so sleek and strong.

I trickled in meat, tiny pieces in a steady stream, that caught in the current, hung in the eddy then trundled off down river along the gravel and sand bar these big fish patrol. The light continued to fall, taking the temperature down with it.

The waterhens were busy, fighting and splashing for roosts, and then, triumphant, their clear calls clucked through the air. A rat ventured out, swimming still tight up and down the far bank. For a spell, the chub were active, humping under the surface, slurping after moths and rummaging into anything that floated above them. Their great amber eyes drew in the light to help them see, and their even greater white lips could feed and probe so sensitively through the weed and flotsam for anything gone astray and still edible.

The lights from the city began to glow against the southern skyline. The arterial roads grew busy with the commuter traffic; planes to the airport lumbered overhead like strange stars of flashing red and green lights. Duck plummeted into the sedge like darts on the breeze. An owl called its heart away in the copse over the river. Life was poised between the natural and the artificial. What I was doing seemed fragile and threatened by civilisation and therefore all the more precious to me.

The float continued to play against the stream. It drifted tirelessly from side to side, dipping sometimes as the unseen underwater currents entwined around the line or shouldered against the lead on the bottom. Each time, I hovered by the rod and then sighed and sent down the dribble of meat once more.

I began to wonder, by six, if she were eating the tiny pieces, or even if she were still there beneath the bushes at all. I had seen her the previous day, her huge dark barbel shape treading water over the lighter gravel bed. I could not guess her size: the water was not clear enough, the sun was low, the light was poor and she was down deep and hardly moving. But I knew she was big. After all, if a barbel looks large, then she will be huge. She will be deep and bullock-shouldered. I have seen enough to know.

Lost there in the marsh, I remembered other barbel nights. Best of all, there was the Severn, that deep, great, green, oily water where the barbel burrow like pigs and bubble like bream, when I fished with Ron Lees and his mate Bob Jones. The beasts there never give up, but go running away into the darkness past the lights of the cruisers and houseboats as though they would never return. Don't I remember Bob's near-despair, watching his rod arch over again as a big fish righted and fled once more from the net? It had been on for hours and he would not land it, if I remember right, till 3 a.m.

One of the few river carp brings me back two hundred miles east to reality as it slobbers for the cheap luncheon meat that has floated into the brushwood in the slack. He is two feet from my feet, coal-black against the grey water. The city, the planes, the owl and all else is forgotten. The world is just me and him, canopied by a bush. Part of me whispers to try for him. Imagine him rising over my bait and the line wriggling and twisting off down the rod. What a fury the strike would bring. Then most of me remembers the black barbel and I fish on for what I came for.

Even a mild March night gets cold. The Barbour had kept in all my body heat. It was as though I was in bed on an icy morning, loath to move, happier to sit snug in the ribcage of trees than to pack, walk and drive home. Lethargy mixed with the hope that the giant creature could still be there, even feeding beneath me.

The rod buckled over and pulled across the branches that supported it. A second of true power hammered the cane round and then it gave in all too quickly. It was a chub, but a fine fish for all that. At four pounds or so I could not really be disappointed, and during the inactive weeks I would think highly enough of him. Still, he had ruined the swim; even the carp had exploded when I struck, so I tackled down and left the wetlands, my heart still beating loud.

THE MORNING KILL

I am wondering how my pike spent the early part of her day, that last Sunday before Christmas 1984.

The night had been without frost, but very dark, so I suppose she had been comatose for long, long hours before the dawn. Light broke slowly, only a gradual paling of the greys over two hours. Probably she began to sense day, and to stir at around 6 a.m., becoming fully alert an hour later.

Certainly she fed some time, for later when she lay momentarily in the keepsack she regurgitated a tiny perch, so fresh you felt you could breathe life into it with ease.

After the perch, or perhaps two of them, she moved steadily on to her prowl, picking up her patrol route along the bars and the troughs that rib the eastern end of the lake. The day was very mild, overcast with periodic rain, and the light remained low through the starkly clear water. This suited her perfectly now she felt hunger. She would come upon her prey from the gloom, like a ghost, grey and mottled dark green, silent and grim. She was death stalking the lake. Anglers on the clubhouse bank noticed that the jacks lay low and wondered if a giant were at work amongst them.

The take!

Similarly, she noticed them, or at least the unaccustomed disturbance in winter of cars pulling in, of spinners spun, of baits cast and splashing close around the banks. I talk of unaccustomed winter disturbance because this is primarily a summer lake; pike fishing is strictly limited.

Like a shadow, a submarine, she moved away, over a hundred yards out by mid-morning, and began to hunt once more.

At ten she came close to an overwintering brown trout. His three pounds would help fill this cavernous, rumbling belly. She needed him badly, not desperately, but when he sensed her and disappeared like the spotted genie in a puff of silt some primeval anger stirred in her. Nothing else must escape. Nothing else would.

By this time, the wind had risen sufficiently to drift my superficially absurd yacht-sailed float to a mind-boggling distance. I was concentrating on an area some hundred and ten yards from the shore. By a happy chance, my bait was a rainbow trout, some eight ounces in weight, alive, but only just after three hours on the hooks. The wind also had hard rain in it. There was a lot of doubt in my mind and I might easily have packed and left.

The she-pike, the water wolf, had readjusted her position to face the oncoming wind currents. She lay on the lee side of a broad gravel plateau, so positioned that her eyes scanned the entire area. More perch had appeared, but veered off again well to her left. A four-pound bream had wandered perilously close, and moved on, free by little more than a length of his anal fin.

At 10.15 a half-dead trout appeared on the gravel bar. His occasionally convulsing belly caught her gaze. He bounced over the sand and shingle. He was almost stopped by remnants of the summer's weed, but he pulled free and continued on his course towards those two cold eyes.

It was now that her fins started to quiver, that the million muscles along her four feet of flank began to twitch, that her gills worked harder as the whole pike's system prepared for a kill. The eyes rolled slowly, measuring the dying trout's course. They clicked computer-sharp messages to the huntress's brain. When the time was right, she drove her body over the gravel sill, took the fish in one and, all within two seconds, sank back into the selfsame nest in the silt that she had left. The job had been done well. She had had practice. She was one of nature's successes.

I saw the float sink.

Hunger forced her to turn the trout quickly and it was well in her mouth when the disturbing pressure, previously unknown, alarmed her. With a thrust of her tail she left the clubhouse bank even further behind, diving blindly into the deep chasm that opened up to receive her.

The twenty-five minutes that followed were the most exhausting of her life. Wherever she lunged, she was brought back up to the light. However she fought away from the clubhouse bank, she was drawn towards it. However deeply she buried into the weed banks, she was prised free once more.

The fish.

Jim Tyree with a super pike from the same lake.

For one of the few times in her life she broke the surface, and felt the spasm of contact with an alien environment. She gasped air. It flooded her body. She had trouble sounding. This dreadful tiredness increased, and in the end she let go her life, letting it fall for the first time into the hands of others.

She weighed thirty-six pounds. I had to place her in a different lake. She spent a little time recovering but made a very sure way into her new world. If I wondered how she spent the first part of that day, I would bet high she sulked the rest.

THE DUEL AT DAWN

The evil-eyed man in grey was already fishing as I looked out at the morning. Possibly he had spent the night in his favourite tree; or perhaps he had come in before dawn. Whatever his movements either way, there he stood by the pond, ill dressed in shabby grey, gaunt against the cold wind.

I watched him a while before going out. Detest him as I do, I have to

My antagonist at home.

admire his quiet, his confidence and his absorbing patience. For ten minutes he did nothing but watch the pool at his feet. The light grew in the sky. The mist smoked more thickly from the water. The birds began first to scuffle and then to sing and then to fly across the valley.

Then he struck. His head daggered down and a mirror carpling of some two or three ounces slid down that long beak, into the even longer gullet and finally into the pit of the heron's stomach.

When the bird began to stalk again, I moved. I knew the creature had intelligence and the sight of me alone would do little to drive him away. Under the bed lies the twelve-bore, both barrels loaded, safety catch firmly on. Those cold eyes that see everything in the bird's universe, above and below the water, picked the gun metal out when I was a hundred yards away. On slow wings, he picked himself out of the bay, climbed and swung northwards.

I could have returned to bed. The bird would not return before evening after such an alarm but, next morning early, I would bet on his presence once more. This time I decided to give chase, not to kill the heron – that would be against the law and my convictions. No, I wanted to hunt him out of his patch to somewhere where he would do less harm. North. He was on a journey to the second of his four fishing grounds, to Farm's Mere.

My van rattled down the track in pursuit. I parked two hundred yards from the pool and slid through the barley field, and up to the 300-year-old Dutch barn. My foe was already fishing; I had been quite forgotten, contemptuously put aside in the bird's confident mind. Angry now, I launched myself from the building, aiming to put a shot across the heron's bows. Crawking with rage, the bird wheeled off over the beet field. I fired high and wide and the explosion cannoned off the walls of the farmyard. A dog barked. Fully committed now, I followed my adversary south.

I knew he was going some two or three miles to the river and I reckoned to get there before him. I drove fast with mounting excitement in my heart and pulled in by the bridge. I ran along the headland and hid amongst the bramble undergrowth at the point where the river widens and shallows over sandbanks and gravel depressions. I picked the place where the heron comes for his small trout, his minnows and anything he can root from under the larger stones.

I was well concealed. Even the glaringly white van was disguised by the spread of a thick alder. The ambush was a good one. I saw him grow larger in the sky, begin to plane and unfurl his lanky legs. He had no suspicion I was there. He was coming down.

I gave him both barrels this time, well wide of the mark but enough now to put terror into his cry. He swerved. I thought he was going to fall, but winging through the willow scrub he made his escape. Alarmed, he disappeared north-east. He was on his way to the moat pool.

I considered. I had the miserable bird who had cost me so many fish on the run. He was worried. It was up to me to make the next move the right one. On this last throw I determined to take my time. I left the van half a mile from the water and crossed a meadow, past the still sleepy cattle. Down the dip and I was into the ooze of the flooded alder carr.

I moved slowly. No branch must crack, no pigeon must startle away. The heron must have no inkling of my approach. I scanned the water each step. He was not there and I feared my knowledge of the bird was incomplete. Still, I edged on.

He *was* on the pool, camouflaged to near-invisibility against the brickwork of the bridge arch. Confident creature, he was slowly wading the shallows with no other thought than the second course of his interrupted breakfast.

But I changed that. I peppered the pool five yards in front of his toes with an 'under and over' of No. 7 shot. The effect was remarkable: he dumped into the water in a tumbledown of rag-bag feathers. For a second I feared that I had done for him, but he reared up and, screeching all the way, he made off over the skyline north-east and out of the estate lands. I hoped for ever.

The day bloomed and passed. Dusk fell and yet, on the point of darkness, the geese cackled and set off the dog. I looked out of the window. Perfectly framed by the rising moon was the heron settling for sleep on his favourite gnarled oak branch. How cruel do you have to be to be kind, I wondered, as I turned off the lamps and went upstairs myself to bed. The morning duel might never have been!

FROM THE GREEN SEA

Already it was the night before the last day, a September night, and darkness came in early. The stars were brilliant for a while over the moors and then, galaxy by galaxy, they were snuffed away by the cloud from the west. Rain fell, heavy from the first drops, and the wind rose, bending the trees on Hawkridge, scattering the first leaves of autumn to the ends of the earth.

Logs hissed in the bar-room hearth, sometimes raised to flame by the blasts that eddied over the mansion and curled down the chimney breast. The fishermen were gathered there, quiet for the most part. Only

Hunting in the shallow water.

occasional sentences studded the silence. One had lost a near-ten-pounder by the boulders. Another had seen fish coming up the falls into the Black Pool. All were agreed that the rain against the window would flood off the saturated moorlands and colour the river long before dawn.

I walked down to the ancient clapper bridge where the water was inky in the lost-star night and a thickening brown in the torch beam. Even through the rain, though, and over the talk of the trees, I heard an owl call, felt there was hope and turned in ready for an early start.

Water gurgled in the gutters. It ran in the drainpipes. But above all sounded the grumble of the rising river over rocks in the Vicarage Pool. Drifting into sleep, I felt water-borne, more fish than man in a world oozing water like a cosmic sponge.

The one lost fish that day haunted me. Close my eyes, and I saw a gleam of disappearing gold. I dreamed then of salmon. *Salar*. The shining fish. The leaper. The death or glory boys. Salmon had become the most emotive word in my language that week – above mother, father, love even. I was a child again in my desire for the fabled fish.

Dawn broke hardly at all: it merely drizzled out into a slowly lightening greyness. Hazes of cloud hung over the ridge, hardly moving in the vanished wind. The gloom struck you to the bone; even the

The glittering Exmoor river.

The grilse in the morning sunlight.

spaniels slept, stretched like antique maps of the world, flecked with continents and half-guessed-at islands.

The amber river showed just enough clarity for me to continue, to take the forest track up the valley, like centuries of travellers before on grizzly Exmoor dawns. A buzzard called high above, drifting like its collective ghost over a lost land.

For two hours I climbed, to the top pools, over rocks greasy with rain, mosses and peppermint lichen. Pools that had been placid only hours before now roared. Shallows that had rippled were now crested like the backs of legendary sea serpents. Only here and there, in useless slacks, could I put a fly before the river grabbed it roughly off its course.

Still, there was hope. The rain had stopped. Patches of blue widened until they spread from ridge to ridge. The sun was warm and by a late lunch the river which had been so quick to flood was proving equally keen to fine away. As I sat over a shallow pool, the lights could pick out the bottom stones – and the pursuit of my day. Through a pane on the water, I glimpsed a salmon, a fish up from the green sea!

The soul of the river.

Salmon! Like father, mother, and love, everyone has his own image. Perhaps it is a grand Scottish river or a sandwich with the crusts cut off. Now mine was of the wayfarer up one of Exmoor's smallest rivers that I was trying to stop with a wand of a trout rod at the closest quarters.

The afternoon lengthened and dusk tiptoed into the shadows of the forest. I set to fish my last pool of the day, of the year come to that. The neck was no good. I heron-walked to the tail and the cast went down. A salmon swished over the fly, so close she must have touched it with her flanks, brushed the nylon with her scales. Same line, same place, second cast and the fish took with total certainty.

Madness broke out in the valley. She blurred silver in sky as much as in water. She took me down the rapids into water waist-deep. I lost my hat, my net and my heartbeat before I beached her a hundred yards down from where she was hooked. It was dark now, but the walk down was easy. I had the soul of the river by the tail.

I passed a farm, lamps lit, where a dog barked at my steps. Salmon jumped occasionally beneath me, safe in black pools, and then the moon raised itself above the ridge and the river glittered away for me to follow home.

SEVENTIES SURVIVORS

Friday night and I walked a stretch of old memories. The Indian summer sun was setting and the floodplains were as lonely and wild as they had been years before. Lapwings, in from northern Europe, called wistfully and geese grazed amidst the cattle. Everything was bathed in tranquillity, in a golden light, and I wandered very happily amidst the ghosts of roach past.

There was the alder where I once took a monster of 2lb 13oz and there the bend that produced eight fish from 2lb 12oz in a week. I walked the straight where I caught my second 'three' to the deep hole that gave me my first. The water-cabbage bed existed still where, nine years ago, I hooked and lost my biggest roach ever, on the rim of the net.

Every yard of water in those two miles held some reminder of fish, weather or companion. There had been little change since those winters of dedication I used to spend there, through wind, rain and snow. Perhaps, I reflected, the major change was in me, in a weakening drive to devote my life to a single species, to tiring nights that would, after all, only be duplicating triumphs.

And there was doubt in my mind, that Friday evening, whether the fish of the past still existed either to the same size or in catchable numbers. In four miles of walking, there was not a roll, a swirl, a splash or a dimple. There were no bubbles, no deep-down gleams, and not a pike strike –

A sleepy floodplain river.

nothing at all to make me want to return with a rod ever again.

Yet, unaccountably, on late Sunday afternoon I arrived ready to fish. I tackled up, cast out and promptly fell fast asleep. For well over two hours I barely moved, apart from to shift the numbness in my arm or swish away a persistent, bothersome fly.

Once there was a heavy splash, forty yards up river, well into mid-stream, and I opened my eyes to squint into the low-lying sun. There were coots about and I thought no more of it but fell back into the grass once more. I was happier with dreams than reality and only woke when the evening air cooled and church bells rang up and down the valley.

Roger Miller appeared in the gloom and we talked whilst the sun finally sank and the hum of insects grew louder than any other sound in the deserted valley world. Sedges were rising off the river in their millions and as we looked upstream they created a haze over the water.

A fish rolled.

It was big. It was silhouetted in a ring of glowing water where I had heard the splash an hour before. Almost immediately, other fish appeared around it, kissing in insects and the hatching nymphs.

We were in a frenzy. Half my brain worked and at least half panicked. I shook so that I could hardly press on the flake and my first cast went wildly astray. Roger threw together his gear, but before he could fish I was into something large. It ran deep for a yard and the hook length broke.

At once the river was quiet again and though we stayed well into darkness there was no further sign of fish. We tackled down and in the still mild evening walked off the floodplains. We talked in the bar. That the fish were roach, there could be no doubt. Chub, bream, trout and all the other possibilities were discounted, not because of wishful thinking but because of the years of experience we could muster.

That the fish were big roach was equally obvious. From the swirls, from the glimpses of backs and tails, from the way they gulped down crusts, they were the standard of fish that we were searching for. Eight, nine and ten years ago, I was catching fish on the fringe of two pounds – not the super roach, but good ones, still young and still growing. The

Fishing the tail of the weir.

shoal that we had found, I figured, were these fish, survivors of the seventies, and possibly huge.

But by now it was late; the night had been frantic and I feared that our imaginations were playing a part, perhaps leading us down rivers of fantasy. We set a meeting there the next night. We blanked. And the next night. And the next. And so the story has gone now for weeks, long past the break-up of the fine autumn, into more typical weather. We have not seen a roach, never mind hook or land one. We have theorised. We have prebaited. We have quivertipped and bobbined. We have trotted. We have used bread, maggot, worm and caster.

Yet I know we will succeed and one glorious fact has emerged since that first Friday evening: I find myself laughing at the trouble, at the walks, at the mud and the wind and rain. My fishing life has been revived by the existence of those survivors. I am, in fact, as keen as I ever was. My enthusiasm too, is a survivor of the seventies.

NIGHT AT THE BOAT-HOUSE LAKE

On the night when the radioactive cloud from the stricken Russian power station drifted over southern England, I went to see the old owner of a large estate near me. It was the first good weather of the year and I drove through countryside busy with tractors at last on the land, ploughing, planting, fertilising, working on until after dusk.

I was shown into the man's study, where he was watching the early evening news. Even though the fallout was over us, the house, the estate, we were made to feel secure. Radiation levels were very low. 'Experts' had said there was no risk to public health. I winced. This is official jargon for any problem, however bad. I counted back the number of times this platitude had come out in the Wensum campaign and how many times I had feared it to be suspect.

We waited until the weather forecast was done with, for, although he is nearly ninety, he still oversees the farm and wanted to plan how work would progress. Then he told me to take a rod and said that we would drive down to the lake.

I call it the Boat-House Lake. He always sits on the veranda of the thatched building and watches me fish for some brown trout he stocked years ago. Most are still alive and, now that he does not carry a rod himself, I believe he likes to see me stalk a rising fish, play it to the net and return it unharmed.

A trout from such a place would taste worse than a bream, for the

A calm evening over still water.

water is muddied by the workings of carp. And there, you guess, my true interest lies.

The breeze was soft, pushing slightly from the south-east, and debris had gathered in a bay by the side of the boat-house. One trout at least was working along its margin, sipping in the flotsam of the day. I snaked out a longish line and let a buzzer lie in the surface film.

I did not work the fly, but rather looked around for signs of the carp. Strangely for estate lake fish, they had never bred and they had, as a result, grown large. I had had one twenty-pounder. It was an old and gnarled mirror with just a few scales along its lateral line, each as big as my fist. It was a very dark fish, all but black, horny, all hoary with age. There are larger fish than him in the Boat-House Lake.

The trout took me with confidence and the leader slipped away into the sunset-streaked water. The old man cheered from the veranda as it hit the surface and threw a cluster of golden droplets. I played it slightly overlong to please the old man, netted it and took it to the boat-house on display.

Just a baby from the Boat-House.

It was a fine trout, slightly big-headed, rather lean, but a very deep yellow and heavily spotted. Its breathing was coming in gasps and the man held it a moment in his crooked arthritic fingers before its return.

Then, for a while, we enjoyed the evening air. The sky was cloudless, the stars came out and the whole evening glowed. One carp head-and-shouldered twenty yards from us. It too looked a dark fish, like jet against the rose-glazed water as it hung there motionless on its pectorals.

I do not know if you have been to the Louvre in Paris to see the *Mona Lisa*, but to watch a rolling carp like this always puts me in mind of that painting. In both, the eyes hold yours and follow you. Both carp and lady seem to exist for only you for that moment in time. Then, both carp and painting are masterpieces and irreplaceable and precious.

We talked about the nuclear cloud. 'I know you are worried,' he said. 'I have lived through two wars and I tell you that nothing is ever as bad as it seems.'

I love old people. They have so much wisdom and experience, but, for the first time in years, there was no comfort in his words. Even though he faced a personal death, the sword of Damocles had never hung over his whole world. No one would envy him his years in the Flanders trenches; he did not know there would be a poppyland waiting for him in Norfolk, should he return. Now, though, it seemed to me that our whole environment could be destroyed, not just individual lives.

It is a very simple pleasure to sit by a lovely lake and admire the beautiful woods and pastures around. To lose that pleasure, not just for myself, but for everyone, for any angler, for all time, seemed impossible to face.

I have got the old man's permission to fish the Boat-House when I want this summer and I will be back and back. Never believe that virgin carp are easy. There are endless challenges there. I want to find their patrol routes and how to wean them off bloodworm and, worse, the daphnia clouds.

I desperately want a very big fish from there, partly for the old man's sake and partly to prove to myself that I have mastered a difficult water. Always at the back of my mind I fear I might not have many years left to me. The carp are old. Their master is old. And who knows what the 1990s will bring?

THE OLD MAN'S JACK!

In the world of piking, there are 'men's' waters and 'boys'' waters. On these men's lakes, the sport is gruelling: the hours are long, the weather is always cruel and the fish are very few. But they are big when they do come and it is this promise that makes those few diehard anglers forsake the boys' waters where the piking is easier and there is always action of some kind.

Without making myself out to be a hero, I confess to love the lure of the hardest waters and there is one pit in particular I go to where legends and records are talked of. It is a devil of a place. It is exposed to every wind and a run a week is not bad going most winters. Despite all this, I am hardly ever alone there. Virtually always an elderly man fishes with me, day in and day out, with a desire for big fish just as bright as mine. Wind, frost, snow, sleet or rain do not deter him from the hunt for monsters. Nothing will, in fact, until death comes to name him. He cannot stop, he says. Ever since childhood he has been pledged to catch the mightiest of pike. He is a man with a score to settle.

He was eight years old and it was Christmas. For a present he was given a fishing holiday on one of our great rivers. He travelled by train with all his luggage and tackle, was picked up by cab and taken to a small-town hotel.

His greatest desire was for a pike and he told the men in the bar that

A good pike powers off.

night of his quest. Plenty of advice came his way, but the voice of one wrinkled ancient rang out above the others. 'Go to the old wharf, boy,' he said. 'Fish in the dock and get a bait down deep. There's a 35-pound jack lives there, lad – believe me, there is! Forget the river. Go to the canal.'

That night the young boy could barely sleep. He could hear the laughter in the bar continue into the early hours but it hardly bothered him. No, his only thoughts were of the great jack in the grey-green water of the canal docks. Wolf-like, its eyes burned at him through the dark of his room. He finally fell into a fitful sleep just before dawn.

He fished all that day down at the canal wharf with all the knowledge and skill he could muster. He caught nothing. His spinner worked hour after hour with no reward. His livebait bobbed at its bung quite unmolested until dusk, when the boy went his subdued way back to the hotel.

That night in the bar it was the same story from the ancient man. 'Oh yes, he's there all right. An evil critter. Head hard as iron. You're not deep enough. You dredge the bottom for old jacks like that one there.' And, so saying, the old sage and his cronies burst once more into laughter.

In shy confusion, the boy left the room. Now he was even more determined to get that great jack and prove his ability to them all. He knew he could do it – but the next day and the next were just as blank as the first had been. He felt no pike, he hooked no pike and he saw no pike there in the brooding waters of the canal.

The boy's last night came round. Howls of laughter greeted his disappointed face. 'No luck again, lad? You know, those old jacks feed rarely. Barely at all at times. Looks like you've hit on him when the varmint's stuck in the mud like some old stick or something. Better luck next year, eh!'

The home train left at lunch time. The boy took his rod down to the wharf that last morning and knew that success lay far away. He was simply going through the motions. Around ten, the barmaid passed him along the towpath and smiled. A few yards on, she paused, stopped and returned to him.

'Look, dear,' she said, 'those old buggers in the hotel have been playing you along all this week. There's no big fish down there – there's nothing in this cut at all, it's been polluted so many times. Come. See what they have been plaguing you with.'

She took his hand and led him up the steps of a tumbledown warehouse. They crouched on the brickwork and she pointed down into the canal basin. In the misty water the boy saw a suspicion of iron and he looked harder. He began to make out the outline of machinery.

'There's your fish, love. A jack. A winch, call it what you will. Daresay it weighs over thirty pounds, but the only time it's ever moved is the day it fell off this wall here. That's what the old devils have been playing you along at. And very proud of themselves they are too to fool a little lad like you!'

God knows how long ago that ill-natured prank took place, but it certainly made its mark. As the boy grew to be a man, the determination for a great pike did not falter. Those old-timers, long since dead, sparked something off that is still being enacted. The boy has become an old man, but he is still there, still on mean waters when the winds howl and the rain comes down like stair rods. And there he will always be until the thirty-pound jack hits his net at the last.

POOL OF PEACE

On a neighbouring estate there is a very old pool, dating back to mid-Victorian times when a stream was dammed across a tiny secluded valley.

There it still hangs, an acre of water up a hillside. There is no house near it, nor any road, and even the bridle-path peters out a field and a copse's length before it. So it is as lost as any place can be today: sometimes there is a shoot along the rough drives, or the smoke of a woodburner's fire, but mostly I know I will be alone.

For that peace, and for its great beauty, I love the pool and try to go there every day. Its surface is the face of a friend, made interesting with constant change, sometimes blue and sometimes grey, sometimes serene and at others ruffled by the winds.

Originally there were sticklebacks in the pools, a few loach and eels that squirmed up the valley watercourse, but there was a lack of big fish to give life and zest to the water. So one summer, in the late afternoon, I carried a great tub of baby carp there. I had no help. The carp sloshed in their tank. The horseflies bit deep and the nettles raged through my shirt. At the dam I finally watched the tiny fish scatter, reform, and – happy again in one, tight body – slip as a shoal away into the cool depths of the pool.

Winter came. There were many clear frozen nights when the big moon lit up all the valley. At those times frost fell a full sixteen hours out of the

One of the fingerlings.

twenty-four, and even in the sunshine the temperature never rose more than a degree above zero. The skim of ice thickened steadily. The winds became easterly and snow fell. The carp were in a tomb as the light in the water faded and the oxygen levels faltered.

For weeks the rabbits and deer of the woodland could walk over the pool and the waterhens froze solid in the sedges. The geese made for the coast and the saltwater dykes and a kingfisher died in a crevice by the outflow.

With the thaw, many of my small carp I found floating in the margins, bleached quite white, dead for weeks. This almost coincided with the snowdrops, and then the bluebells pushed through the mosses around the birch trees. The toads appeared at the pool one day and for two weeks thousands of them mated amongst the rushes and yellow flag.

Summer came in and settled down very hot. The feeder stream grew thin, trickled and almost died. The level of the pool dropped, leaving its tidemark around the dam wall and the mudbanks exposed like hump-backed whales. In the deep central channel algal blooms developed and a lime-green scum spread cancerously as the sun shone on.

The carp that had survived the winter grew on fast. They ate the

A quiet corner amidst the willows.

emerging tadpoles and bubbled endlessly amongst the bloodworms. The entire stock seemed to be fully scaled commons and one leather, now. All the baby mirrors had died under the ice.

A storm came one night, with thunder, wind and more than an inch of rain. The old shooters' hide was destroyed, an oak fell and the dam was partially breached by the rush of water. More carp, I fear were lost down the valley where they could never survive in the little rock pools.

And then it was autumn and the birch leaves fell and all but covered the pool before they sank, rotted and added to the silt. I saw the carp shoal for the last time in October, when the fish came up to some floating pellets. The leather was still there. There were eight commons. They were all that survived through that first year out of the hundred and seventy that I had stocked.

All this is several years ago now and I have had no desire to catch the carp, only to watch them and feed them, and probably because of this relatively untroubled existence their growth rate has been rapid. The leather especially has got on well and recently I decided to have him out for a check on his weight.

Of course, he was easy to hook, but he fought like the very devil. I let him lie on the weeds as I slipped the barbless number 4 from his bottom lip. I eased the damp weigh sling under him, recorded just over ten pounds, and he was back within a minute, feeding once again the following day.

Without the long-dead squire, there would have been no pool, and without me, no carp in it. What I have attempted, individuals and clubs are doing the country over, benefitting the sport that has given us so much.

It is a trend which I hope swells everywhere, for what so many of today's non-angling conservationists do not realise is how much our inland waters need fishermen for their preservation and development. We are creators, not destroyers.

THE BLUE DART

All summer long a kingfisher lived on the ponds close by me. He fed all the hours of light on the carp fry, which he took to his nest by the outfall pipe. He raised his family and stayed on into autumn and early winter, struggling now with the carplings and preferring the plentiful sticklebacks.

Right into the new year, his thin piping cry echoed up and down the

A period of cruel frosts.

valley. He sat on the alder trees, on the bridge and on the gently falling willows. He could still hunt and the plop of his emerald body continually rippled the chilled lake.

Then came the freeze.

In the early hours of 12 January a crippling frost fell over the valley and by dawn the pools were ice-free only where the springs were at their strongest. It had snowed heavily and the white mantle from the wood was criss-crossed by the tracks of animals and birds that had come to drink there. Throughout the bitter day, temperatures remained well below freezing and the warm spring-water smoked where it met the Siberian air. The kingfisher flew periodically through the day and caught fish enough to see him into 13 January.

This was the day of the heavy snowfall. From late morning the sky became heavy, groaned and shed its endless white load. The day was dark by two in the afternoon and the wood and the meadows lay in ever-deepening silence. There was no engine noise above all the white land. The snow muffled every sound. The kingfisher lay under its shroud, listening for the crush of fox paw to come at dusk.

On 14 January the winds began to rise. Strong to gale they came from the north-east, sweeping the snows before them. Still the springs kept some water free and now came a great army of refugees for its warmth. A score of waterhens gathered around the deep banks. Ducks and geese came in from the coast and dropped down where the ice-free water winked in the shelter of the wood.

Their wings shook the snow from the long marsh grasses and a dozen types of finch flocked in to feed off the freshly exposed seeds. Their activity was viewed from upon high by a great predator, itself on the move from the gales. It settled on the uppermost branches of an oak tree and watched the activity at the springs. For an hour it was still as carved marble, then it swooped in a purple haze.

The finches fell onto the snow and into the grasses as the sparrowhawk wheeled inches above them. The hawk saw the kingfisher, rose, and fell with renewed speed towards the branch where he sat. The blue bird piped in terror and skimmed away across the ice with the sparrowhawk in pursuit. They whooped around the islands, under the trees and across the bridge and away into the mists of blowing snow. I saw neither of them again that day.

By 15 January it seemed that the sparrowhawk had moved on. The kingfisher, though, was back by the springs. Feeding, for him, was impossible. The shallow water was clouded by the mass of waterfowl and when I threw down sprats they were eaten by the ducks or by the big rainbow trout drawn towards the light and oxygen. I saw no more of him

The Blue Dart.

by midday. His branch was empty right until the early dusk.

There was the slightest thaw on 16 January. That and the commotion of the wildfowl had opened the clear water still further, but the kingfisher did not reappear. I fed the water liberally with grain, biscuits and bread and watched the birds fight with the fish for food. Even a couple of good commons had come up from the deeper water to join the faster rainbows. They raised showers of bubbles over sunken wheat and sucked at bread slipped under the ice-pack.

The wind had quite gone and the day became almost mild. I felt we had to venture through the woods and out across the meadows to the village for some supplies. We left in the mid-morning but the drifts were piled high down all the avenues in the low-lying coverts. We broke out on to the fields where the snow had been scraped nearly clear by the winds and where we could make our way a little more easily. Down in a hollow stood the shepherd's cottage, still locked in by the ocean of white. His dogs barked as we passed on the skyline.

The village had been blocked for four days and supplies in the shop were limited. Even the pub shelves were all but bare. We went out in the thin afternoon sunshine, to the river, to see the horses by the mill. Half the water there was iced over, but along the rapid shallows it still twinkled along quite free. The thaw had not coloured the stream and the tiny brown trout, dace, roach and gudgeon were lying plain against the gravels. I even fed them pinches of bread from what must have been one of the last loaves in the village.

Quite suddenly, it happened. In a volley of sound and colour our kingfishers sped upstream, saw me and bolted into the alder thicket. A big red sun broke through the clouds to the west, and for a moment I felt blissfully warmed. I had not gone fifty yards when I heard the splash of the birds fishing again, of nature once more looking after her own.

THE FINAL PRESENT

The day had seemed endlessly long: tedious phone calls to ageing aunts, kisses forced by a mother-in-law, a strained present giving when nobody had received what they wanted but put on shallow faces of sincerity. Lunch was late. The turkey was unpleasantly dry. The fire was uncomfortably warm. His wife had been hurt when he received his gift rod ungraciously and now there was a sullen atmosphere between the two of them.

And all the time the day outside had moved smoothly along without him from promise to perfection: a cloudy morning; a rising wind to a steady force 4, from the south-west at that; a drizzle at noon and a light intermittent rain soon after. If a day spelled pike, not turkey, it was this miserable birthdate of Christ.

Tempers finally exploded about three o'clock over something as insignificant as a small, slippery plate in the kitchen. Bending over the shattered pieces, her face looked up at him, beautiful even now in the tears. 'Get out. Get out. Go on to your lake and leave us all alone.'

He needed no second bidding. Rather ashamed, he avoided the looks of the family and got to the car – always loaded in case. The engine took some starting, and half-way down the drive he stopped and went back in. He picked up the new rod and a trace of a smile crept over his wife's face and then froze over as he half slammed the door in a repeated goodbye.

His self-pity increased on the way to the lake. The depression had obviously been a small one. Even as he drove, there was no more need for the windscreen wipers, as the sky cleared in enormous sweeps above him. But the heater fan was on. It was growing rapidly colder. There was condensation on the rear window, the rain fallen on the verges was beginning to crystallise into an early frost.

He could have wept from the frustration of the whole day. He very nearly stopped and turned back – but then the rough track was only a mile away and the thought of the Queen and ever more food spurred him on. It would, after all, be good just to be alone, to clear the noise, his headache, the excess of spirits, alcohol and bad temper.

In the hut, dark against the sky, a light shone. Amazingly, on that day, he was not alone. He ran through the club membership in his head and could not think who would be out on Christmas Day. He went in. It was only some old-timer.

There had never been much closeness between him and this man, one of the founder members. It had always seemed from their gear and approach that they were miles apart – at least the three generations of time between them showed in everything they did. And yet the older man's face shone at the sight of him and, though it was the last thing our hero wanted, he could not reject the offered cup of cooling, oversweet tea.

Our hero – the time has come to give him a name, so let us say John – threw together his gear. He looked at the new rod and put it down again, unthreaded against the shed. The old man picked it up. 'What a lovely rod,' he said. 'I can see why you don't want to risk spoiling it. Look at those whippings – and the fittings too.'

'They're not even Fujis,' John muttered. 'There will be a night's work for me changing those.'

'Oh yes, but it will be worth it for a rod like this,' the old man replied.

The old man already had his baits working in the area John had wanted to concentrate on, but, of course, a request to share the patch was not refused. So, together, they sat on the veranda of the hut, watching their floats against the water. John had, naturally, way outcast the old man with his superior strength and tackle, so the whole area was being covered to at least eighty yards out.

It really was a marvellous evening. They were looking right into the deep red sunset and, while John cursed it as a forerunner of a cold night and a bright day to follow, the old man enthused on the glory of God and the natural world. Duck hissed in towards the islands and geese whooped in the eerily stark spaces overhead. Small fish flipped all over the lake like rain and here and there pike erupted amongst them and the golden water spewed and foamed like a land of volcanoes.

John had a run. His float travelled five yards west, dipping all the way into the sun. The young man wound down and walked backwards tightening hard into the fish way out. His rod took on a hoop and

As the sun set the line began to tighten.

juddered, and the battle was on. It was obvious to both men that the pike was a good one and when it tailwalked over a distant ledge, splendidly etched against the flame sky, even the experienced old man grew excited.

The fish rose again – up, up – and both men could count the seconds of its flight. As it hung there like a fabled bird, it lashed its head and the bait catapulted like a splinter, into the void. The fish hit the surface in a roar and that dreamlike moment was over.

John hurled the rod down the gravel bank. He cursed his mother, his father, the stars at his birth and his miserable Christmas. The old man tried hard to comfort him. He rightly said how hard it is to judge the weight of a fish at a distance. He said the day was not yet over and perhaps more big fish were on the prowl. He insisted that there were worse things in life than a lost pike. He took from his pocket a most fine hip flask and poured John a measure of brandy into its ornate silver cup.

The younger man leaned, half exhausted, against the hut as the old companion retrieved his rod and wound in the chewed bait and frayed trace. John was now so truly miserable that all the anger had gone out of him. He handed back the shining flask, admitting that something, still, could be beautiful on such a grim night.

'It was my wife's last present to me,' the old man said. 'It was

A battle rages.

Christmas ten years ago and she died in the January, a week before our anniversary. I said there were worse things than a lost pike. Wait till you lose your wife and then you will know. There is no one for me to go home to. There is no one to listen to my joys or sorrows any more. There is no one to let me out on a Christmas Day – no one to buy me a new rod like yours. But enough of my goings on, though – I'm only trying to cheer you up. Let's finish off the brandy and have our last casts.'

They did. They stood together by the edge of the darkening lake as the stars came out and the fish movement gradually ceased around them. This, at last, was peace. This was the tranquillity after you have cried, or been in pain and relief has flooded back to make the unpleasantness only a memory.

One of the old man's rods was on the move – the one that John had secretly laughed at an hour before, cast a couple of yards into the margin. He got down awkwardly to the rod and for the first time John realised just how old his partner that night was.

This fish, too, was very big. For minutes it did nothing but keep its position fifteen feet down and make the old cane creak like a mast before the storm. Then it ran and its run was the escape of a bull and its pace forced the wooden centre-pin to give line to the backing.

Who knows how long the old man fought the giant under the rising moon? Who bothers to time a struggle that enters the annals of history? From where did the aged body find the reserves of strength to lean into the pike as it did and how many years had it taken to build up the experience that guided the fish from snag out of snag?

John, at first impressed, now felt wonder, and then awe at the ability of such a fisherman. Never had he appreciated what true skill involved until that Christmas night. The profile of the old man's face, the angle of his body would stay with him for always.

At last the fish broke surface in a heavy ripple – not yet beaten, but recognising its master. The old man turned to John; 'You take the rod. I've had enough.' John refused. The old man put the rod into the reeds and walked away towards the hut. The line tightened. The rod pulled into the water and John was forced to take up the rod and join the fight himself.

At once, the old man was back at his side, advising and encouraging, alight with the drama of the struggle. The ancient tackle worked wonders in John's hands and the cane had qualities he had never guessed at, never even read of, and soon the pike would be his. The old man squatted against the waterline, the net well sunk. 'Keep it coming. Keep it coming. Head up. Line tight. Keep it coming, boy' – and in a cascade of black and silver water the pike was on the land.

They staggered to the hut and weighed, measured and photographed her under the light there. Never had John felt such a moment. He felt giddy. He had to sit on the bench a while to recover.

The pike went back. The old man's tail-lights disappeared up the track and John was alone again by the lake. It could all have been a dream, but for the footprints in the frost, the exposed film canister in his pocket and the traces of blood from a cut from the pike's tooth. The whole day stretched out before him. He relived every moment, good and bad, and became increasingly aware that he hardly deserved his magnificent reward.

Home was in darkness. His wife was alone sleeping in front of the fire, the flames playing on her hair, her face, her long pale neck and delicate arms. He knelt by her and kissed her and told her every detail of the great day.

She listened and put all the right questions – what bait, what size hooks, and so on – and then, in a small voice, asked how the new rod was.

Mean but magnificent.

'It's perfect. Absolutely perfect. There's no work to be done at all.'
'So it won't need to go back then?'

'No, it won't. I don't think I understood it at first. It was all my fault. It's the ideal rod. I have just realised all of it . . .'

'I am glad you went. Pike, men and Christmas go together, don't they?'

'Yes, *but* you should have said that pike, Christmas and *sportsmen* go together.'

They laughed, happy together in the warmth of Christmas.

DECADE CONCLUSION

A fisherman's past is never totally lost and gone. There must always remain memories of people, of waters, of things learnt and of all the heartbreaks suffered. As I write now, though, the future dominates once more. I am done looking into history when there is so much to be attempted in the fishing world. As each decade draws to a close, another potentially quite as rich seems to open out before me.

The watercourse I follow seems never-ending. I want to catch salmon, silver fresh-run fish from spirited rivers under mountains capped still with spring snow. I plan to tangle with the predators of the lochs of Scotland and Ireland. Lomond in winter, Mask under stormy western skies and wild pike hooked in deep, endlessly clear water are what I want

Reg Sandys, Billy Giles, John Bailey and Roger Miller – anglers older and younger.

now. I am dreaming of more barbel, more sea trout and more fish that fight their hearts out in the lost lonely waters of Europe.

Perhaps this all sounds like a fantasy, but I have the time, and certainly the will, to make the romances come true. When the fish exist, you will catch them if you want them enough.

There are two men who together reinforce my hope that the future can be at least as glittering as the past. I fish with Bill and Reg for a few days each year. The one is retired, the other is well into his seventies. They have been partners for over thirty years, have never fallen apart and are inseparable to the day I write. They have both caught huge fish and are legends in the piking world.

Despite all this, their enthusiasm is undimmed. They are out early. They stay late into cold December nights. They appreciate every fish they catch. They applaud the captures of others. There is no jealousy and no spite. Their adventures continue. There is no standing still for them. Game fishing in Scotland, piking in Lomond, piking in Russia, trouting in Canada – all lie on their horizons now. A whole life at the waterside lies behind them and yet the future ticks on in an alarm clock set for four in the morning and another piker's dawn.